RODERIC BARRETT

RODERIC BARRETT

by David Buckman

Foreword by Thomas Puttfarken

Ahead of the Light by Hal Bishop

A Chappel Galleries Publication

First published 2003 in Great Britain by © Chappel Galleries

© Images Lorna Barrett
Paintings, Drawings and Prints by Roderic Barrett unless stated otherwise
© Foreword Thomas Puttfarken, Professor of Art History & Theory, University of Essex
© Introduction and Biography by David Buckman
© Ahead of the Light Hal Bishop
Photography by Doug Atfield (see Further Acknowledgements)

British Library Cataloguing in Publication Data
A catalogue record for this book is available from the British Library

ISBN 0-9545327-1-6

Editor: Edna Battye

Printed by Alphaprint (Colchester) Ltd

Chappel
Galleries
Fine Art

15 Colchester Road, Chappel, Essex CO6 2DE
Tele and fax: +44 (0)1206 240326

Front cover: The Good Samaritan 1997–2000 by Roderic Barrett
Back cover: Brown Bird (c.1950) by Roderic Barrett
Frontispiece: Roderic Barrett 28.2.37
Endpiece: Roderic Barrett in his Studio 1996

CONTENTS

FOREWORD

Ever since Roderic Barrett established himself in the early fifties as a serious painter he developed not only a personal, distinct style — simple and clear, mostly with subdued colours, sparse yet at the same time of immense compositional intricacy — but also his own subject matter. His pictorial worlds are inhabited by a range of recurring figures and objects, not of a realistic or naturalistic kind, but generic in nature, types rather than individuals. Paintings of the 80s and 90s, like *Players* (1981–84) or *Remembered Bedtime* (1993–96), show female figures, small girls or mothers, who belong clearly to the same family as those in early works from the 50s, like *Family Breakfast* (c.1954) or *Familiars* (1954–56). Prominent among Roderic's protagonists were always children and the poor, the ill, the dying and the bereaved. Other favourites are clowns and circus artistes, with the circus and the stage as traditional metaphors of the world. Here we also find actors playing oppressors, hypocrites and charlatans. And then there are the occasional figures borrowed from mythology, like gloomy fates with threatening scissors or sinister angels with dark wings. A mystical unicorn makes rare appearances. The worlds these figures live in are defined not in traditional terms of pictorial space, like landscapes or interiors; instead we may find rather flat abstract shapes that act as a ground in front of which the figures' environment is defined by a few objects, chairs, candles and buckets, if required a table or a bed. A simple horizontal line may substitute for the horizon. There is no doubt that all of these items have profound significance in Roderic's work. We may not be able to capture their precise significance with words, yet objects and figures clearly constitute a kind of visual vocabulary, or a pictorial language of symbols, allegories and metaphors.

Roderic himself was not prepared to translate this visual language of his into words. It was notoriously difficult to get him to talk about the meaning of his pictures. In his view the subject-matter of his art was simply there, it was an undeniable part of life itself, of the human world. In his experience of the world there were profoundly personal traumas, like the early death of his mother, which contributed to his lifelong melancholic predisposition. Other experiences were more generally of the times — the years of WWII, the shadow of the nuclear bomb, the Vietnam war. And then — even more generally — there were the seemingly endless miseries of the human condition: poverty, illness and death, only occasionally alleviated by a spark of hope against the odds. These were the things that troubled Roderic's mind and his sense of humanity; it was the stuff that, in a better world, should have been the object of all serious intellectual and artistic endeavour, of philosophy as well as of poetry, of music as much as of painting. There was a clear sense of moral duty for Roderic — for reasons of personal background and upbringing to be discussed later on in this book — to address these issues of human suffering, frailty, and injustice. And this he did initially with few, later with no concessions to the fashionable activities of the contemporary art scene, the gesturing, branding and re-branding of avant-garde and cutting edge artists of his own and subsequent generations.

In terms of subject-matter, then, of meaning or 'messages', or whatever we want to call the content of Roderic's visual speech, he did not speak the prevailing visual language of the second half of the twentieth century. Instead he belonged to a tradition which, in the first half of the century, was represented by artists like the mystical early Chagall, the Picasso of *Guernica,* and the Beckmann of the Great War and of later triptychs. Yet he is also part of a much longer line of earlier masters like the Goya of the *Caprichos* and the *Disasters of War*, or the *pinturas negras*; or even earlier still the late Titian who, in the only idiom then available outside that of religious painting, that of mythological scenes, presented the tragic sufferings of the humans at the hand of the fates and the gods in such famous pictures as the *Death of Actaeon* or the *Flaying of Marsyas*.

While Roderic's subject-matter, the content of his paintings, is of a general, even universal nature, it is his 'formalism', his insistence on precise pictorial composition, that marks him out as an artist of his own century. And this aspect of his art was something he talked about with great passion. Human suffering, fear and hope are not in themselves artistic, they need to be transformed into a formal structure through which they acquire their specific visual meaning. Where the poet uses words, rhymes, verses and rhythms within the overall structure of a poem, in order to give poetic sense to his subject-matter, so the painter uses lines, shapes, colours and grounds within the overall structure of his picture.

Roderic's pictures are intensely structured, very precisely

composed. Abstract art of the first half of the century had certainly been a formative influence on him, the 'classical modernists' like Mondrian and Kandinsky rather than the contemporaneous abstract expressionists in the United States or the *tachistes* in France. How one shape or form stands in relation to another, and how all of them stand in relation to the whole was of crucial importance for Roderic's sense of the success – or otherwise – of a painting. And the same is true of the relationship between figures and ground: in some compositions, like the late *Song and Dance* (1994–97), the ground with its own vibrancy and luminosity becomes an active and central player with the figures dancing within and around it. Elsewhere a large area of 'empty' ground is balanced against a densely composed arrangement of figures and objects (as in *Table with Man*, 1995–96). I feel that Gestalt psychology, with its emphasis on the whole as the defining force of our perception, as formulated in the widely read books by Rudolf Arnheim and others in the 50s and 60s, provides the closest theoretical parallel to Roderic's thinking. I have found no reference to it in his own short treatise on pictorial composition, but I suspect that both Roderic and Arnheim drew on the same formal traditions of the earlier years of the century.

But in the end he was not a formalist, even if he sounded like one when he talked about painting, and even if some of his pictures, in particular still lives, look remarkably like exercises in abstract art. He was undeniably attracted to abstraction. It was his deep sense of moral obligation, I think, which kept him from actually becoming, like so many of his contemporaries, an abstract painter. Pictorial composition was the crucial means through which pictures could work, yet it could not be an end in itself. For a person of Roderic's nature and upbringing, a socialist and pacifist, himself often haunted by the 'black dog' of melancholy, the main theme and indeed the very end of art had to be man. Even his still lifes are about man, snuffed out candles are obviously about death, as in *Candles for Dead Friends* (1977–80); empty chairs, particularly when they have been knocked over, imply previous – and perhaps suddenly interrupted – presence, as do empty but battered pails and dustbin lids.

Given the emotive charge of his subject-matter the viewer is never in any doubt that Roderic's art is not primarily about formal unity in the sense of merely abstract relationships of shapes: it is about the genuine expression of emotions and feelings filtered through a comprehensive mastery of pictorial composition. For him the 'formal' positioning of each figure and object in an overall whole was decisively dependent upon their emotional demands within the pictorial context. And these demands Roderic would respond to and express, not in words or rational thought, but in visual arrangement, order and emphasis. Whether a young girl occupies the very centre of the stage, as in *Players*, or a marginal one, as in *Hauntings* (1987–91), or even one where she is half cut off by the frame, as in *Song and Dance*, defines in very important, yet entirely visual ways, her emotional relationship with the other figures and objects within the whole work. We become aware of the importance of these relationships when we realise that otherwise there is very little interaction between the figures in any given scene; the pictures do not tell stories in the traditional sense of narrative art. The expressiveness of Roderic's figures is normally not geared towards a common action but towards a prevailing sentiment.

A point Roderic himself liked to make was that what mattered in art was not originality but authenticity, not 'the shock of the new' but 'the getting it right'. For him this was a moral issue as much as an aesthetic one, and it could take him years to develop a composition to the level where he himself felt satisfied that he had 'got it right'. Yet even then he could change his mind; given the chance he would rework and 'correct' or 'reform' earlier pictures if he found them wanting later in life. Emotional honesty and hard work characterise his art. Spontaneous outpourings, improvisation and grand gestures are notable by their absence. It has to be said that this did not make him popular with art critics and dealers. He was aware of this, yet throughout his long career he remained unwilling to compromise.

Thomas Puttfarken
Professor of Art History & Theory
University of Essex

AUTHOR'S ACKNOWLEDGEMENTS

Writing about Roderic Barrett has only been made possible through the help of some who knew him. Lorna, the late Hugh, Jonathan, Mark and Kristin Barrett shared their memories. The interviews that Joan Ellis made with Roderic for the project Colchester Recalled were invaluable. I have also had helpful input from Michael Barrett, Charles Debenham, Andrew Dodds, Cynthia Copnall, Peter Freeth, Susan-Jayne Hocking, Edna Battye and Waj Mirecki, Ron Sims, Robin Warnes and Rachel Widdows. Katy Munro, at Moorfields Eye Hospital, also provided information.

AUTHOR'S BIOGRAPHICAL NOTES

David Buckman has been a full-time journalist for almost 40 years, initially on the staff of several magazines. Working for an American-owned energy monthly, he travelled widely in Europe, Africa, the Middle East and South-East Asia. As a freelance, he wrote for dozens of British and foreign publications and made several hundred radio and television broadcasts. After the 1998 appearance of his *Dictionary of Artists in Britain since 1945*, the standard biographical work on the period, he has written full-time on art. He contributed to Macmillan's 28-volume *The Dictionary of Art*. Artists' monographs include J B Manson, Leonid Pasternak, Jonathan Clarke, Mary Griffiths and Martin Leman; *Mixed Palette*, a study of Frank Ward and Kathleen Walne; and *Charles Debenham's East Anglia*; and he lately completed a biography of the sculptor A H Gerrard. He writes frequently for *The Independent*.

FURTHER ACKNOWLEDGEMENTS

I wish to thank Lorna Barrett and her family, as sponsors, for their co-operation in publishing this book on Roderic Barrett's work spanning seven decades.

Thank you very much to David Buckman for his detailed biography of Roderic Barrett, involving interviews, visits and research. Thank you also to Thomas Puttfarken for his penetrating Foreword; Hal Bishop's inventory of Roderic Barrett's Prints 1934–56 and the essay on Barrett's wood engravings: Ahead of the Light.

Photography: principal contributors Doug Atfield, Michael Barrett, Eddy Van Helfteren, Janus Van Helfteren, Peter Winwood, with much appreciation to Doug Atfield for the co-ordination of photography and commitment to the project.

Picture credits: Anglia Television – *page 42*; Beecroft Art Gallery, Essex – *Plate 89*; Chelmsford Museums – *Plate 106*; Colchester Art Society – *Plate 44*; England & Co – *Plates 7, 8*; Epping Forest District Museum – *Plate 163*; firstsite, Colchester – *Plates 107, 187* and *photograph Roderic Barrett in his studio 1996*; The Redfern Gallery – *Plate 118*; Angela Godfrey *Page 39* Playhouse Gallery; Simon Hilton – *Plates 4, 105*; The Executor of John Farleigh – *Page 28 'Melancholia'*; and others who have given their permission for their photographs to be used in the book; special thanks to Elizabeth Routley.

Information and assistance: Bristol Museums and Art Gallery; Chelmsford Museums; Christchurch Mansion, Ipswich; firstsite, Colchester; Free Painters and Sculptors; Gainsborough's House, Sudbury; Norwich Castle Museum; Philips Exeter Academy USA; Royal Academy of Art, London; Tate, London; University of Essex; University of Glasgow; Victoria University of Manchester; Victoria and Albert Museum; Victor Batte-Lay Trust; Courtauld Institute of Art; Alan Ellis, Colchester Art Society Hon. Sec.; Stephanie Collier, Waj Mirecki, Sandra Pepper, Fred Robinson, John Sansom.

Production: Matt Lippert, Bob Newell, Jane Rogers

Edna Battye, Editor

INTRODUCTION

Roderic Barrett was a perfectionist, restlessly unsatisfied with the image he created even if he had worked on it for years. Owners of his pictures and dealers in them were sometimes asked by the artist to borrow back work so that he could amend it. If they granted permission, when it was returned any change to the canvas might seem undetectable, but not to the man wielding the brush. "I see my paintings in different surroundings and they seem quite different," Barrett told an interviewer in 1967. He was then in mid-career, when he might have been expected to be assured, at the height of his powers. "I am continually trying to alter and improve things. I can't stand still."

As a young wood engraver or later as a painter producing large canvases, Barrett consistently produced singular and often disturbing images. It is understandable if the viewer is mystified by Roderic's personal iconography. What is the meaning of these assemblages of clowns, skulls and grotesques, candles and half-candles, unoccupied chairs, scissors, jugs, bowls, dustbin lids and hoops, butterflies and coats, wheelbarrows and drums, pails and playing cards? The picture titles, of jam-pot label simplicity, give little away.

Roderic was not necessarily much help in explaining things. His wife Lorna remembers him after completing a picture saying: "I still don't know what it's about." But then, as Picasso said: "Everyone wants to 'understand' art. Why not try to understand the song of a bird?"

"Painting is a hard and cruel world," Barrett said in his late forties. "It doesn't matter what you do, in the end all your emotional and technical inadequacies will be revealed. You're committing yourself whether you like it or not." By then, he had experienced much of the world's cruelty at first hand. This, combined with his own nature and the legacies of a singular family history, contributed to works that are unmistakable and unique. His are some of the most memorable and powerful pictures in twentieth-century British art.

CHAPTER ONE

FAMILY BACKGROUND

Roderic Westwood Barrett was born in Salisbury Avenue, in Colchester, on January 8, 1920, into a vigorous family with a long radical tradition. The elements of this family background and his childhood experiences are essential to the understanding of Roderic's later approach to the world.

His father and grandfather were also both born in the Essex town, his great-grandfather, William, eventually working there, although stemming from Warwickshire. By trade, William was a tailor, by conviction a nonconformist radical and Chartist.

Chartism was a working-class movement, essentially the product of economic depression, which took its name from a People's Charter demanding such reforms as manhood suffrage and secret ballot. Although it formally lasted only from 1836 to 1848, it acted as a beacon for the later trade unions and the Labour Party and was remembered for the organisation of marches and monster petitions. William helped form the Tailors' Association of Colchester, was mentioned in the Chartist press as an organiser of collections to support the families of imprisoned Chartists and went on working for its ideals through the Working Man's Association, Colchester Amalgamated Tailors' Association, Colchester Association of Engineers and the Farm Workers' Union.

The radical group to which William belonged subscribed to publications carrying the writings of Karl Marx, whose *Communist Manifesto*, written in collaboration with Friedrich Engels, was published in 1848. Following the influx of refugees in that year from the various revolutions in Europe, William was among those who attempted to form an international association which would prevent worker from fighting worker. Roderic remained "inordinately proud" of his great-grandfather, "because he tried".

His son, Roderic's grandfather, was also a tailor whose tailoring business, employing a few men, mostly catered for the gentry and comfortably off middle classes. He was named William O'Connor Barrett after the fiery Chartist leader Feargus O'Connor, but was more cautious than his father, being a Liberal and active Congregationalist. Roderic was fond of him, remembering him as "not an altogether sweet-tempered man. His use of language was in the tradition of Dr Samuel Johnson. Where a long word was possible a shorter one would not be used." William O'Connor was in the fine tradition of Barrett characters. Roderic recalled that he smoked a pipe, drank a pint of beer every day, ate Spanish onions and black, rock-hard liquorice which was strong, dark and bitter.

Two of William O'Connor's passions were walking and choral music. Once, when Roderic's brother, the asthmatic Hugh, was 11, he and grandfather "walked from Colchester to Stoke-by-Nayland and back in the same day, which was a good 30 miles." At the age of 80, grandfather celebrated by walking 80 miles. He sang bass and was conductor of the Colchester Choral Society for many years. William O'Connor devoutly believed in Bach, Schubert and Handel, *The Messiah* being for him the crowning glory of all choral music. There was a strong Barrett tradition of family music-making, Grandad Barrett holding musical evenings at End Cottage, Lexden. "He had false teeth, which were forever clicking against the stem of his pipe. They were so likely to drop down and nearly out that he removed them before he began to sing, placing them on top of the piano. This seemed to me natural and not at all an odd thing to do," Roderic recalled in a short memoir penned in old age.

Fiery radicalism and nonconformity was a strong thread on the maternal side of the family, too. Roderic's great-grandmother Mary Elliot, "a small lady with one leg shorter than the other," whose radical father was famed for making "straights" – boots which could be worn on either foot – and who took his pigs for a daily walk in Hadleigh High Street, was an eloquent lay preacher. "Powerful on sin she was, so that when in full spate her audience groaned with horror at the depth and depravity of their sins."

Roderic's father, Cecil, was to carry on the family tradition of nonconformity, not least in his many-faceted and enterprising career. One of 13 children, he was born in Colchester and, aged 14, was apprenticed to a firm of ironmongers. Although he survived well into the twentieth century, his memories were of an age long past. As a boy, there would be a surge of excitement in the town when the Royal Mail coach arrived, having travelled on the gravelled road from Ipswich. On market day there was a stall for an itinerant dentist, whose assistant blew a trumpet vigorously to smother the yells of whoever was having a tooth extracted without anaesthetic.

Cecil met his future wife Edith Janet Harper, always known as Janet, while skating, during a severe winter when the ponds were frozen over. After marriage, Cecil was set up by his father with an ironmonger's shop in Eltham, Kent, where Roderic's two much older brothers, Alex and O'Connor, were born. With his next shop, in Farnham, Surrey, he added a horse and van for rural sales of paraffin, pails, brushes and so on, finally taking another shop in Colchester.

Cecil was a steady presence in the Barrett family, a sweet-natured optimist if not a natural businessman, who believed that there was good in everyone. Later, he would give unfailing support to his sons in their careers.

When his third son, Hugh, announced a new venture, having been in and out of jobs, "That sounds like a good wheeze," was Cecil's response. He was an energetic man, known as Cocky Barrett, recalled Roderic, with "a fair whack of belief in himself," who found great excitement in new ideas and activities. A propagandist for the Labour Party, Cecil was also keenly interested in the liberal educational ideas of A S Neill, founder of Summerhill, new notions of monetary reform and Social Credit and ethics gleaned from Tolstoy and the *New Testament*. He was undeterred when his attempt to set up a housing association was foiled by a combination of estate agents and solicitors.

While living in Eltham, Cecil joined the equivalent of the World War I Home Guard, but when he was asked to charge with a fixed bayonet at bag of straw set up to represent the enemy, he could not do it. On his return to Colchester, he became a member of Headgate Congregational Chapel and a Sunday School superintendent, his developing pacifist beliefs being shared by the pastor Roderic Dunkerly. It was after this minister that Cecil's fourth and youngest son, Roderic, was named. Like the pastor and his father, Barrett was to be imbued with lifelong Socialist and pacifist convictions. Although he had no belief in God, he had "an enormous aversion to the idea of people killing each other, which I find quite grotesque."

Early drawing of his father, Cecil

CHAPTER TWO

SCHOOLING

Within a year of Roderic's birth in 1920, his family had moved from Colchester to a three-acre market garden at Church Lane, Lexden. His two much older brothers Alex, born 1904, and Oliver O'Connor, born 1908, were now much senior to Roderic and Hugh, who had been born in 1917. Roderic hero-worshipped all three older brothers, Hugh's companionship remaining a key influence throughout his life.

Cecil's pacifist convictions had prompted the Lexden move. With the introduction of World War I full conscription in 1916, Cecil refused military service. This led to his being court-martialled, sentenced to prison, released and served his papers again under the cat-and-mouse tactics that were used against militant Suffragists. Although he was not brutally treated, Cecil did suffer extensive imprisonment which brought him into contact with the philosopher Bertrand Russell and Socialist activist Fenner Brockway, whose ideas he respected. He also had the opportunity to read widely. At home, in the evenings, Alex and O'Connor were giving moral support by posting pacifist/Socialist pamphlets through local letter-boxes.

Without Cecil to run the hardware shop, it had to be sold. Still under sentence but out of prison, Cecil was set to work in greenhouses. It was this experience that he decided to exploit on three acres at Lexden, where he built a bungalow and grew salad and soft fruit. Although there were proceeds from the sale of the ironmongery shop, it is probable that Janet's father helped with money to buy the smallholding. He was a ship's chief engineer, on the Bristol–China run. The Edinburgh-based Harper family, however, included a fair sprinkling of dour doctors, lawyers and clerics, Janet's great-uncle being the principal of a theological college who merited "an ugly granite plinth inscribed lengthily in Latin." When Grandad Harper retired from the sea, he opened a wine bar in Colchester, operated as a wine merchant and bought some small houses in the town. Janet was his only child and sole beneficiary.

Roderic remembered how hard it was for his father to work the weed-infested land with a spade, but for himself and his brother Hugh, "apart from his appalling attacks of asthma, it was an idyllic life. There was a dirt lane just outside the garden, along which the farmer from Prettygate Farm trundled his horse and cart and then, apart from a few houses, there was nothing but trees and fields." Cecil kept goats, "Greyling and Betsy, who were gentle and beautiful, and Billy, who was handsome, touchy and stank. There were also springy, delightful kids to wonder at. As goats didn't give enough milk all year round, the pleasure of drinking goats' milk was followed by what at first was the unpleasant taste of cows' milk, which initially was just as distasteful."

A wire-haired fox terrier, Bob, entered the family during Roderic's first year, an inseparable companion whose only vice was to fight and kill a local Great Dane. Thus, Bob "had his chest ripped open which had to have stitches. During the following night he pulled them all out. We were very proud of him for doing this." There were chickens and two Spanish long-legged, smooth-coated donkeys, Jack and Flossie, "with the most elegant thin-lined cross in black along the back and down the shoulders. Hugh and I used to ride them bridleless until we fell off." They would pull a high-wheeled cart laden with produce into Colchester market. "Attached to the trap was a hooter which when squeezed made a noise like a donkey braying."

After a term or so at Lexden School, aged five Roderic with Hugh was moved to Stanway School. "It was very strict. We all sat at desks, very still and any inattention was rewarded by a sharp rap over the knuckles with a ruler. We chanted our tables and copied copper-plate letters from a book. Boys also did horticulture, digging and planting. The only exciting occasions were holding a ribbon and dancing round the maypole to form a colourful pattern on the pole, and Empire Day. That stood out because with much seriousness each of us was given an orange, fruit that otherwise we only ate at Christmas. Was I unhappy there? I think I was just too frightened to do anything but toe the line.

"It was whilst at school that the appalling thought came over me that I'd have to go through all this again. Where the notion of some form of reincarnation came from is a mystery, but the dismay I felt at the time remains clear."

With children now ferried quite small distances to and from school by car and contemporary concerns about personal hygiene and educational facilities, the journey that Roderic and Hugh made daily in the mid-1920s and what they faced when they arrived seem a stark contrast. "We walked from Lexden to Stanway School, I then five years old, a good two miles there and back in all weathers. I remember how important it was to relieve ourselves on the way, as the only latrines at school were earth closets that stank. This was no hardship, as we were accustomed to and preferred squatting in some handy place, preferably near dock leaves to wipe ourselves with.

"Stanway School had some rough children and parents. Although I had an older brother, I could look after myself and was very aggressive. During playtime there were often fierce and bloody fist fights, mostly between the Union, or Poor House, boys and boys from ordinary homes. The Union boys wore brownish corduroy shorts and smelt of carbolic soap. Although Hugh and I wore boots with metal studs in toe and heel and corduroy shorts which were then regarded as very working-class, we felt our shorts to be altogether superior because the material was well thought of at home!"

Although he was only to know her for a few years, Roderic's mother and the domestic life she created were to make impressions that would resonate in his mature pictures. "My mother was the world in which I lived," he wrote in old age. "There was the closeness with Hugh and the rather more distant one with my father and elder brothers, but the surrounding and all-enveloping atmosphere was the presence of my mother. She didn't raise her voice or slap, but, because of what she was, generated a very firm sense of what to her was right and wrong. Perhaps because unspoken, it made her influence all the more powerful. By nature she was undemonstrative, no doubt reinforced by her Calvinistic religious upbringing." He even spoke of her "Scots fierceness".

The centre of Janet's domain was the kitchen, with its cast-iron, black coal-fired range on which all cooking was done, summer or winter, creating an atmosphere of comfort and warmth. There, Janet would darn by the light of an Aladdin oil lamp. "Having undressed in the warm kitchen, Hugh and I made our way to cold beds by candle light. Only now, some 70 years later, am I consciously aware of where so often candles in my paintings come from." There was a fondly remembered bedtime ritual. Roderic, Hugh and mother would then sing a hymn. "We said a prayer together, which was followed by our asking that the bedroom and sitting room doors be left open so that we could hear her playing the piano, Chopin, Schumann or Schubert. What a powerful combination: mother, religion, music — an inescapable memory.

After this it was story time. Hugh would start off an adventure which would then be taken up by me. This would go on turn and turn about until sleepiness overcame talk." (below: drawing 1948 and plate 252 Christmas Card wood engraving)

CHAPTER THREE

LETCHWORTH

In 1929, the Barretts moved to Letchworth, in Hertfordshire, where, just over a quarter of a century before, the first Garden City had been begun to the design of the architects Parker & Unwin. Cecil Barrett himself liked starting new ventures, so he went into business with a friend in Letchworth, while retaining his land in Colchester, on which he was to build houses.

By the time of the Letchworth move, Cecil had become a Quaker. Roderic and Hugh were accepted as day boys at St Christopher's School. A fee-paying boarding school run by a Quaker headmaster along semi-progressive lines, it was supported by many wealthy parents, although Roderic remembered that Cecil's more straitened circumstances were accommodated. "It was a good middle-class compromise between regimentation and the freedom of somewhere like A S Neill's Summerhill. There was a sort of uniform, grey shorts and sandals. If you wore anything other than sandals, you were an outsider. Remember, this was George Bernard Shaw country.

"I went from a school where fisticuffs were normal to somewhere where all fighting was verbal. If you really wanted to hurt somebody, what you needed at St Christopher's was a good vocabulary. I had a lovely time there, with two very good friends, and ended up being left very much to my own devices, doing a bit of biology and history, otherwise art almost all the week." The influences of Cecil, Roderic's older brother Connor and a good art master all helped here. "I was pig-headed. I had a blind need to paint and draw, and nothing was going to get in my way."

By the time the Barretts were settled in Letchworth, the two older brothers were well on the way to establishing their careers. Alex, referred to by Hugh as the only "normal" brother, studied to be a teacher at Borough Road, the Isleworth training college, and eventually became a very successful headmaster in local authority schools in Hertfordshire. The brothers all reacted differently to home and church influences. Roderic remembered that "Alex aged seven shut himself in the lavatory and said in a clear voice 'God does not exist!', and waited for some response from above. When there was none, he felt that that was that and was in this matter troubled no further." That, too, was the conclusion that Roderic himself adopted.

Connor, like Roderic an artist, was to become a professional sculptor who also wrote poetry and composed music, a legacy of his early family life. He studied at art school in Colchester and Ipswich, then developed his carving technique with Tibbenham's, an Ipswich firm that made furniture as well as ecclesiastical sculptures. He went on to exhibit widely, in England and America, eventually returning to live in Colchester and then Wales. His highly stylised figures, such as *The Crucifixion of Mankind*, in Colchester Public Library, are not unlike those in Roderic's wood engravings and paintings. The *Crucifixion* was one of the illustrations in Connor's 1980 privately published book *Myself Emerging*. The title made Roderic squirm. By that time Connor was dislodged from the pedestal on which he had earlier placed him. "He liked to be worshipped, I liked to worship, and it was wrong for us both," Roderic said in a late interview, but he conceded that "you may not like what he does, but he's a beautiful craftsman." Against Hugh's and Roderic's atheism, "all his life Connor was a believer in a wide range of notions: the artist as prophet, Unidentified Flying Objects and the healing power of various therapies."

Hugh left school in 1933, after spending much of his time at St Christopher's in the library, to begin a remarkably enterprising career, initially working as a farm pupil, then as a farm manager. From 1953, he built a serious reputation as a broadcaster and scriptwriter, mostly on agricultural subjects, for BBC home and overseas services. From 1968, he lectured in Tanzania, and then worked for various government and non-government agencies abroad before returning to England. His autobiographical volumes *Early to Rise*, 1967, and *A Good Living*, 2000, are minor classics. He was – and had to be – the most commercially shrewd of the brothers. Roderic believed that Hugh "was some sort of Pantheist, certainly he did not believe literally in the Bible, more a physical/mystical relationship with the natural world."

The much older Alex and Connor "were a source of wonder and excitement when they came back for holidays. Alex was teaching in London. They enlarged our small world, with their talk of religion and politics. They were creators: furniture – only oak was acceptable, book binding, carving panels and drawing. All this was much encouraged by the William Morris Arts and Crafts Movement. It was proper to do and to make, not buy, if possible."

The older brothers fostered, with Roderic's parents, his love of the arts and curiosity about them. In words that he left to be read out at his funeral, Roderic emphasised that, as well as being "grateful for the hours spent making paintings," he was "grateful for the poetry and music that were never outside what I have been." Shakespeare's Sonnet 116 – "Let me not to the marriage of true minds" – was read there and the music chosen indicated his diverse interests, developed from the classics played late at night by his mother: part of Bach's *Fourth Brandenburg Concerto*, a Haydn trio and Louis Armstrong's *What a Wonderful World*, with accompanying lyrics. Later, his musical tastes ranged from the Beatles to Prokofiev and Stravinsky.

Continuing the Barrett family interest in choral and vocal music, Cecil sang while Janet played the piano. Roderic remembered Connor "standing heroically with his violin and Alex making wild and agonising faces as he played the cello. Alex brought home the first records we ever had: Dvorak's *New World* and Schubert's *Unfinished Symphony*. One of the things that absolutely entranced me was that they played all the early Beethoven trios, his violin and piano sonatas as well as Schubert. It was something that I never had too much of. Mother, Alex and Connor made watercolour paintings influenced by Dvorak."

Roderic's daughter Kristin recalls that even though Roderic when married did not have much money for material things, "he would find it for something like learning to play the piano. He was a good pianist and had a wonderful grand piano on permanent loan from a friend, John Bullough, a bachelor friend living in Boxted." John Bullough was originally a friend of Roderic's older brothers, a collector of his work and, because of his involvement with the Sudbury firm Agricultural Contractors Ltd, was to commission Roderic to illustrate its catalogues for a number of years.

Roderic's childhood idyll was shattered soon after the move to Letchworth when, early one morning, his mother died. "I was woken by the sound of my father howling." Hugh saw the body, Roderic never did, and after the event, "it was very difficult to see what was left for me." He had had an inkling of what her departure meant when he was very small and playing while Janet Barrett was washing up. Suddenly, the hooters went to mark the annual Remembrance Day two minutes silence. "I had been about to say something when I was firmly shushed. She simply withdrew even more completely than if she had walked out of the kitchen and gone away. I felt completely abandoned."

Once his mother was dead, Hugh and Roderic were whisked out of the house to stay with friends. "With the logic of a ten-year-old, I refused to believe that she was dead. Having seen in chapel that 'The Wages of Sin is Death', and knowing that my mother was not a sinner, she could not be dead. I didn't tell even Hugh that I believed this, and over the years it must just have slid away. Many years later I told my father this and he was horrified." The incident contributed to Roderic's mature belief that much of the word of God as preached was "mainly dangerous rubbish."

Any woman hoping to replace Janet in Roderic's life would in the ensuing years clearly be in for a hard time. His wife Lorna recalls Janet's reputation for never expressing irritation. "Roderic said that he had never seen her angry which, as you can imagine, left me in a spot." With such an idealised maternal background in his mind, it is not surprising that when Roderic married Lorna, the joining together of two positive characters, there would inevitably be frictions.

When Roderic's stepmother came along, there was friction, too. Cecil married Winifred about five years after Janet died. It took a long time for Hugh and Roderic to accept her, although Lorna and the family remember her as a delightful woman, outgoing with a good sense of humour, but very different from Janet.

His mother's death did not turn Roderic into a misogynist, quite the contrary. Interviewed towards the end of his life he several times insisted on talking about "the women in my life." These were recalled fondly in details, including childhood sweethearts long remembered from his days at Stanway School and St Christopher's.

CHAPTER FOUR

STUDENT AT THE CENTRAL

When he was still only 15, Roderic left St Christopher's School and began to look for a place at art school. "A mixture of arrogance on my part and the persistence of my father made me reject the one at St Albans and another. Then we heard through St Christopher's that the Central School of Arts and Crafts, in London, was a good place. We went to see the principal, but he said: 'No, there's no place for him, he's not 16 yet and he's not been to a previous art school.' But my father said: 'Well, we are here, and I would like to show you his work.' That was it. They took me, having swept some regulations under the carpet."

Some pictures survive from Roderic's days at St Christopher's, completed in his early teens. An interesting example is *Ascension*, of 1933, one of a group of visionary, quasi-religious works. What he produced in future would be transformed by his years at the Central, where he came under the influence of some charismatic and influential teachers.

Initially, Roderic was enrolled in the sculpture class at the Central, being still in awe of his brother Connor, who was by then practising as a sculptor. Lorna Barrett recalls that it was Cecil who insisted on a change of direction. "His father was willing to go a certain way, but he said: 'It will be too difficult to earn a living as a sculptor. Do book illustration.'" Before long, however, he came to the conclusion that he would best express himself in two-dimensional media with more workaday potential.

The Central had been established about 40 years before Roderic joined it. Its early directors, the sculptor George Frampton and the architect W R Lethaby, were both members of the Art Workers' Guild, and it retained an Arts and Crafts Movement flavour in sympathy with Roderic's family background. Unlike the Slade School of Fine Art or the Royal Academy Schools, the emphasis was less on fine art, more on vocational arts and crafts.

Ascension 1933

Early works

Hugh Copnall with Roderic Barrett
January 1938

By the time that Roderic was a member of the student body, Cecil was back in Colchester, building houses. As houses were completed, the Barretts would move on. Each day, Roderic cycled to the station, left his bicycle and took the train to the Central. "After I had been there a while, I was advised to apply for a Major County Award, and I got £50 a year. Because I wanted to do other things in London, during term I took a room." Altogether, he had about £75 a year for room, food and materials.

He and Hugh Copnall shared a room for a time. "We had a pail for the clean water and a pail for the dirty water and there was a tap on the landing. There was a family above us, another family next door to us, there was one toilet down in the basement and there was a bath that took the skin off your bum it was so rough. We had a meal of beans on toast one day, egg on toast the next. I was too young. The weekends I found desperately, desperately lonely."

Hubert – known as Hugh – Copnall would eventually become a farmer while continuing to paint. He was the younger brother of the notable sculptor Bainbridge Copnall, whom he assisted with some of his major London commissions. Roderic's brother Hugh later commissioned a portrait of Roderic by Hugh Copnall. It was a good likeness, although Hugh Barrett saw an element in it of the "town hall portrait".

Early works
Top right-hand image of bowman verso plate 8

Pas Seul 1943 oil
Depicted in the wood engraving The Painter (Plate 266)

Roderic was at the Central from 1936 to 1940, three days a week life drawing and two wood engraving. "In my youthful arrogance I told them that I was not going to draw from casts, but they said that students were no longer required to do that any more. Drawing from casts is sensible, of course, because they don't move, and sculpture tends to sort out the planes for you a bit." In William Roberts and Bernard Meninsky he had two superb draughtsmen teachers, although he later thought that the life drawing teaching was "not very good." William Roberts could draw so assuredly that "he could start off at the eyeball and know where the feet were coming." But there was no explanation from this notoriously taciturn man, "and you can do with explanation." Meninsky was more friendly, but was similarly enclosed and self-possessed.

A self-portrait by Roderic exists from the Central School years. (Plate 1) In the idealised smoothness of its contours, it indicates the strong influence of Roberts, who was to become famous for his rounded, rather tube-like figures.

Roderic was grateful for his engraving teacher John Farleigh, who a few years before had illustrated George Bernard Shaw's book *Adventures of a Black Girl in Search of God*. Farleigh had been an apprentice "and had come up the right way, a superb craftsman. If you gave him a big block and asked him to cut a diagonal, he would do it undeviatingly. When I was a student at the Central, before it went upmarket, they still had apprentices learning printing, who had enormous skill. When the machine was set up and it came down and kissed the block and went up again, printing black without a line missing, it was magic, just magic." While at the Central, he also completed "a few life paintings, a couple of lithographs and an etching." At home, he concentrated on painting, "feeling that part of me should be kept away from art school. If I didn't complete quite a few paintings, things were getting slow!"

Early work

CHAPTER FIVE

WARTIME PACIFISM

With the start of World War II, Roderic's time at the Central came to an end. Three of the Barrett brothers, who all held pacifist beliefs, had to choose whether to serve in the forces or conscientiously object. Connor, in America, avoided facing a tribunal. Alex, over age and a teacher, and Hugh, a farm manager, were directed to continue with their work, but Roderic "expected some form of imprisonment. Religious arguments were much more likely to be accepted than political ones. There were always those awkward words that could be quoted from the *New Testament*, the clear directives from the teaching of Jesus, 'Thou shalt not kill', and such."

Roderic had no strong Christian belief to cite as the reason for his refusal to put on a uniform, but Christ's intention seemed obvious to him. Cecil's experiences in World War I had made a profound impression and indelible in his memory were those two minutes of silence standing at the sink with his mother. Then there was the influence of writers and poets of the period associated with the war, such as Henry Williamson, Max Plowman, Wilfred Owen, Robert Graves and Siegfried Sassoon. Roderic had soaked up their autobiographical writings and poems while at the Central. "I felt it would be a betrayal of them personally, after what they had written, to go to war. My first wood engravings when a student included images of dead soldiers hanging on barbed wire. That war had a terrible fascination for me." (Plate 239)

Roderic went before a tribunal during the phoney war period. "As I was green and not able to conceive of any compromise, I said when questioned that I would not accept any alternative to military service, such as being sent down a mine, working on the land or in heavy rescue, and so I expected some form of imprisonment. When they gave me complete exemption, I had the wind taken out of my sails. I was not going to be a glorious martyr. The worst part of it was that I was being separated from all of those who shared a common purpose."

For a time Roderic helped Hugh on the land. When the bombing of London began, he heard that his teacher brother Alex at weekends was working with the Friends' War Victims Relief Committee at a shelter in Bethnal Green and needed help. Apart from running some schooling and a children's play group, the main job was taking a van with food and drinks to shelters early in the morning and at supper time. In one huge warehouse cellar over 1,000 men, women and children slept. "There were just buckets as latrines. The stench from these, the bodies and bedclothes was thick. The difficult part wasn't driving the van through the rubble, fires and broken glass, but not throwing up when entering this shelter."

Being a conscientious objector cost Roderic no friends, and there was no adverse reaction from the people in the shelters, "just thanks, and a friendly feeling, with mutual help." There were other compensations. Very good entertainers appeared to amuse the people. He and the other helpers lived in a house in Bethnal Green. "One of the young men in our group had a few records, which I played over and over: Rachmaninov's *Second Piano Concerto* and Prokofiev's *Second Violin Concerto*, which is still with me, a wonderful work." There was one ugly incident in the shelter which prompted abuse that Roderic remembered vividly. "A group of clerics came in to give a service. It was then that a number of East End young men, due for their calling-up papers, jeered and shouted them down. Oddly enough I was shocked, which was a bizarre reaction from one who had for nearly all churchmen and what they said a feeling of revulsion."

Despite all the casualties and the standing on a roof and seeing London ablaze, he was not frightened. "The thought of being buried alive *was* very disturbing, and I was more at ease sleeping on the top floor. My main overriding response as the weeks went by was to believe that it would be a good thing if we were all killed. What the human race was doing seemed so awful that it would be best to wipe it all out and start again, a cleansing. Although I was well-versed in the First World War and the Spanish Civil War, I didn't think that all that would happen again, a romantic view."

Both World Wars spurred artists officially and unofficially to record what was happening around them. For Roderic, the scenes he saw left him in a quandary. "When I was in the shelter I saw many things I wished to record. Some of the scenes were enormously touching, a sea of people jam-packed with one or two corridors between them. They would be covered up with odd things. I always remember a small child's foot sticking out from under a blanket. In the evening in the shelter, I drew from memory. To draw on the spot would have been an intrusion." Lorna remembers how later Roderic "said that he thought Henry Moore's wartime shelter drawings were excellent, although he did not like his sculpture."

Eventually, official groups of people were organised to handle relief and the Friends' effort was disbanded. Roderic put an advertisement in *The New Statesman and Nation* and was offered a job teaching art and games at a boarding school in Maidenhead many of whose pupils had parents who were abroad and which took many Jewish children. "Eventually I was teaching everything except French to a class whose ages ranged from five-and-a-half to 11 and I was a housemaster. It was called Maidenhead College, and I had expected a gravel drive leading to a magnificent house. When I arrived, I found that the other two members of staff had also just arrived. The three of us established a record by staying just two terms.

"It was run by a man called Mr O'Higgins. His previous job had been supervising navvies building railways in South America by riding around on a horse with a whip and a revolver. He ran the school on not-dissimilar lines. He and his Belgian wife were drunk almost every night. I never saw any parents while I was there. Many of the children were frightened, the little ones wetting their beds. Yet I had some good times there, I liked the five O'Higgins sons, enjoyed teaching sport and was young and glad to be active and useful."

Shelter   1943   watercolour   35 x 25cm

CHAPTER SIX

FARMING INTERLUDE

By the time that Roderic had completed his two terms at Maidenhead College, his brother Hugh was involved with a number of conscientious objectors in a pacifist, Socialist community at a big house in Langham, in Essex, called The Oaks. Hugh originally heard about Langham from his father, visited the house one weekend and met his future wife, Deirdre, there. It was one of a number of such idealistic communities established in East Anglia around this time and numbered, according to Hugh, "about 20 or 30 people." They were offshoots of the Adelphi Centre established before the war by John Middleton Murry the writer. Murry had founded *The Adelphi* magazine in 1923, the year his wife, the short story writer Katherine Mansfield, had died.

Before the war, Roderic and Lorna, whom he was to marry in 1943, would cycle out to the Adelphi Centre from Colchester, to hear lectures by people such as the sculptor Eric Gill. As well as aspiring to be a leftist-oriented intellectual powerhouse, the Adelphi Centre was a socially beneficent organisation, taking in Basque refugees from the Spanish Civil War and early evacuees from London.

Cynthia Copnall, wife of Hugh with whom Roderic had shared a room when they were both students at the Central, was at Langham and recalls Roderic pursuing his painting there. "He was forever closeted away in an upstairs room in a small cottage…. I found, when he emerged to help out with, say, the threshing of the corn, he was a pleasure to work with and an asset to the concerted effort. Had he not been exempt, but had had to work on the land, I often felt life might have been easier, his spirits lighter. [At Langham] he was so thrown in on himself, but he was always a very likeable fellow."

Hugh Barrett thought Murry's lectures at Langham "wonderful", but "I disliked him intensely … the meanest man on earth." As an offshoot from Langham, Murry aspired to set up a similar farm, which he did, at Thelnetham, in Suffolk. Roderic, Lorna to whom he was now married, his

brother Hugh and Deirdre chose to join the other offshoot from Langham nearby, at Frating. In common with most Utopias, this community eventually became riven by the problems faced by groups of idealists of varying practicality forced to face the facts of daily graft and communal life.

It had been in 1937 when Roderic's father was building houses in Richardson Walk, Colchester, that one of them had been rented by Lorna's family which caused her and Roderic to meet. Her father, Josiah Blackmore, had been a Christian missionary in Algeria before the family moved to England. Lorna attended the High School in Colchester. It was only then that she began to use English as a first language, her native tongue being French. Roderic became very friendly with Lorna's brother Frank and thus Lorna. Early in the war, with Colchester partly evacuated, Lorna was sent to live with her sister in America and attended Wellesley College. Josiah Blackmore went there to lecture. Later, in the war she wanted to return to be with Roderic, was able to get a passage and began nursing at Colchester Hospital.

Roderic and Lorna had about three years at the Frating settlement. It was there that, in 1944, their first child, Jonathan, was born. "I was absolutely a fish out of water, the wrong material altogether," Roderic recalled. After a time sharing a farm cottage with Trevor and Enid Howard, who had to climb to their bedroom using a chair on a table and a hole in the ceiling to avoid having to go through Roderic and Lorna's bedroom, they moved into a converted shed. This had oil lamps, a tiny stove and an open fireplace for cooking. Trevor would be ordained in the Church of England, later serving for many years as Honorary Canon of Chelmsford Cathedral, and they would remain lifelong friends. Roderic remembered Lorna as being "very happy at Frating. She is basically a pioneer, someone who would have been suited if she had set out into the wilderness and built her own cabin.

"The Frating idea was that everybody would get the same wage and work on the farm. Hugh was a sort of farm manager, the only one there with farming experience. Land was cheap then, because of the pre-war slump in farming. There was a weekly meeting where things were sorted out. For some people, it was a godsend. I was supposed to be the resident artist – talk about clouds in the sky! Lorna and I also helped on the land, which I have always enjoyed doing."

The community at Frating numbered about 30, including children. It was a big farm, eventually successful, labour-intensive, with a tractor and seven horses. Those who had a little money, like the Barretts, invested capital, drawing out a few pounds a week, others with no money being paid a wage. Roderic, who needed time on his own to work, found some of the close personal relationships claustrophobic.

Frating Barn   c.1940   watercolour   36 x 52cm

"The trouble with Frating was that it was made up of individualists, who were there because they were all odd bods. They included some lovely people, but there was inevitable wrangling, because there was no disciplined structure. You can all get the same wage, but what if some families have children and some don't? What happens when some members have wealthy families able to give presents and some don't? Sex was another live issue. There was also trouble establishing a pecking order."

Eventually, bitter disagreements led to the community asking Lorna and Roderic to leave. Hugh left not long after, to farm elsewhere. Lorna found leaving Frating "very, very hard, because I loved the place and it was ideal for children. We had very interesting visitors, such as Shirley Williams, the politician, and Alexander Gibson, the Scottish conductor, and Roger Bannister, the first sub-four minute miler. Being forced to leave, we were unable to retrieve the money we had invested. Our friends Trevor and Enid Howard lent us money to tide us over." After Frating, Roderic said that he had "a worse opinion of myself and my fellow human beings than I had in London in the shelters. It took me a long time to regain any confidence in myself as a person."

The Barretts lived here and there in Colchester, with the assistance of parents, until Cecil helped them build a house in Prettygate Road. Roderic's own career had not been neglected at Frating. The community used to put on theatricals in a beautiful old barn, and there would be visiting appearances from people such as the artist Lucian Freud's actress companion. Roderic set himself to draw the barn and write its history for a book. It was an aborted scheme, some of the drawings eventually being given to the eye surgeon John Dobree.

Like his father Cecil, Roderic could be unworldly about money. After leaving the community at Frating Hall, he was for a time without employment. "While he was naturally worrying what was going to happen, he was determined that he would not take a regular job," Lorna remembers. "When I suggested that perhaps I should earn some money, he insisted that he was 'not going to have my wife going out to work!' while I sneaked out on my bike to do evening lessons, and that sort of thing. Only a few years before he died, he came in one day, ranting, saying: 'Why weren't you out earning more money?' It was always difficult to fit money into Roderic's scheme of things. He was really quite unstreetwise and shopping was always very painful for him."

Eventually, Roderic's very good references from the Central School, in London, enabled him to start teaching locally. For a time he taught art at Clacton High School. Although he got on well with the children, the atmosphere of divide and rule among the staff was not to his liking and he was happy to leave. The Barretts' shaky finances were then boosted by his part-time teaching at Colchester School of Art.

The Colchester school in the years after World War II was a good place to teach and study. In the late 1940s, it attracted John O'Connor as principal, other teachers including Blair Hughes-Stanton, Hugh Cronyn and Carel Weight. It was still an intimately small school, with a few staff, its student body of around three dozen being predominantly women, with an injection of men demobilised from the forces. Specialist classes might be only half-a-dozen strong. The biggest ones took place in the evening.

At Colchester, teachers such as Roderic and his friend Henry Collins had to be versatile. "Henry taught lettering and probably a certain amount of graphic design and I helped him with book illustration. I knew quite a lot about layout for a book, the Central having been very hot on that. I also taught life drawing and painting, but they were ancillary. The emphasis was on useful skills, which would help students to get jobs, such as typography, advertising and drawings for textiles."

CHAPTER SEVEN

TEACHING AT THE CENTRAL

Through the post one day came a letter from the wood engraver John Farleigh, head of the book production department at the Central School, asking Roderic if he would like to return there to teach. Farleigh remembered that, like himself, Barrett had become under his pre-war tuition a very skilled craftsman. "Bless his heart! He thought I would be a fitting member of his staff. It had never occurred to me to apply. I had never dreamt of teaching there. Farleigh had this conviction that drawing and design were the same thing. So when I was a student he saw to it that I not only had a day in his department, but one in Jimmy Grant's painting and drawing department, which was wonderful. I remain enormously grateful to Farleigh, Grant and William Roberts."

"When I joined the Central in 1947, I was put into a class with William Roberts, who had taught me. Roberts was by this time a very distinguished figure who had been an Official War Artist in the First World War with paintings in the Imperial War Museum, illustrated T E Lawrence's *Seven Pillars of Wisdom* and so on – but he never said a word. In class, he would tap you on the shoulder, you would get up from your donkey, he would sit down and make a drawing for you, a head or a leg, say. Roberts could empty a class in no time at all, because people didn't know what to make of somebody who didn't talk. But I chatter. I got on well with him. I had shown him paintings when I was a student, because he knew that I admired him, and that is always the way to somebody's heart.

"When Roberts made you a drawing, he did it with as much attention as if he had been making it for himself. There were some lazy people teaching drawing who just did diagrams, and I could do diagrams." Lorna Barrett recalls how Roderic remained "quite fierce about students learning to draw, even when later it became regarded by some as old hat. He would say: 'Well, until they have learnt how to draw a body I can't know what they are seeing in their mind. They've got to be able to draw what their inner vision is.'" Lorna says that Roderic always enjoyed the feedback from his students, but he found it hard work. "Several of them said to me: 'You know, we've got no-one else who teaches one-to-one like he does'."

She believes that it was "almost a physical necessity" for Roderic to have a sketch-book handy, in the evening, while listening to the radio or watching television. His beautifully drawn Christmas cards were collected by friends. Exquisite watercolours, drawings and wood engravings of plants featured for years in the 1950s and 1960s in the calendars of the Sudbury firm Agricultural Contractors Ltd. In a world where the bottom line is now dominant, the trouble that this firm took with the 1951 calendar in overcoming reproductive problems to match in the printed version the quality of Roderic's six original engravings seems amazing. The eventual calendar was so late that it had to be remodelled to cover the period July 1951 to June 1952. Agricultural Contractors even offered "a few hand-made impressions from the original engravings … of these beautiful pictures." (below: drawings from ACL Calendar 1960)

As a draughtsman, Roderic remained open-minded about new materials. His daughter Kristin – the second of Roderic and Lorna's three children, the youngest being Mark – recalls how his drawings "became much more colourful when he discovered felt tips. I gave him a packet and he just loved it. You didn't get red, blue and so on, but a range of colours. Every time it was somebody's birthday in the family he made a card for them. The cards were often based on lettering, as some of his Christmas cards were, but very, very colourful."

Barrett taught one day a week and one evening life drawing, one day design. "You didn't get paid an extravagant amount, but Lorna and I lived on it. She was a good manager, and our expectations were not all that great. The good thing about the Central was that they recognised that, for most artists, they had to teach. You could not do two days at the Central and two somewhere else, so my connection with Colchester School of Art was severed, but, in my opinion, that was a proper discipline."

Reviewing his 21 years' teaching at the Central, Roderic was critical of its direction at points, notably the way in which Farleigh was forced to exit, although his replacement, the industrial designer Jesse Collins, Barrett grew "to love and respect" as a colleague. Collins thought sufficiently highly of Roderic to own his work. A first-hand account of Barrett as a Central teacher and another view of Farleigh comes from Andrew Dodds, who became Roderic's life-long friend. Dodds as a young student had become familiar with Roderic's work in the Colchester Art Society exhibitions, but it was not until after his Royal Navy National Service that he met him at the Central in 1949 when he joined the illustration class which he and Farleigh tutored.

Farleigh Dodds found "rather grand. He proposed all the projects and gave pompous criticisms," with frequent references to his Shaw engravings "and his friends the Sitwells. Farleigh did no one-to-one teaching (apart from four pretty girls), and I cannot recall he ever said a word to me.

"Roderic did all the teaching. He diligently saw every student for at least 15 minutes for a real heart to heart discussion, each class. I am indebted to him for those tutorials because he taught me how to compose a picture. I can hear him now. 'Why did you do that, Andrew? Wouldn't it be better if…' He also taught me to ask those questions of myself.

"At least 70 per cent of students had served during the war and were determined to make the most of this period. Most of the staff, apart from heads of departments, were practising professionals, teaching one or two days a week: well-known artists like John Minton, Keith Vaughan, Mervyn Peake, Patrick Heron, Ruskin Spear, R S Badmin and Bernard Meninsky, to name a few. This talented staff all had conflicting opinions. Students were supposed to be mature enough to decide from whom they sought help. I got a lot of advice from Minton, Spear, Badmin, Meninsky and Roderic.

"Roderic knew I was a country boy and my main subject interests were rural. He respected this and encouraged me in that direction, but insisted on a high standard of design and composition whatever I drew. I left the Central to become a freelance illustrator, working regularly for the *Radio Times* and other magazines, book publishers and newspapers, all with strict time limitations, but I always tried to be mindful of Roderic's words."

Reflecting late in life on his early days at the Central, Roderic realised that it was "only when I began teaching that I realised what the problems were. When you start teaching you have to be able to verbalise and know what you are talking about."

Dressing the Millstones (April)

The Dowser (May)

The Wheelwright's Shop (2) (November)

CHAPTER EIGHT

PRINTMAKING

Although Barrett as a student at the Central had been introduced to the techniques of etching and lithography, as a printmaker it was engraving on wood that preoccupied him until he gave it up in the 1950s because it strained his eyes too much. His prints were of the white line variety, in which shape and strength of cut are governed by the tool used. He liked to preserve some of the identity of the virgin boxwood block, with large areas of untouched black. Barrett "adored" cutting into the end-grain of hard box, which this craft required, and he delighted in the handling of black and white and grey. Even though his paintings are notable for their use of sombre colour, he remarked that "There's nothing like a printed black. You cannot arrive at it in a painting; it has a different kind of body."

Barrett's output as a wood engraver was achieved over a relatively short period but remains an important feature of his work. He began studying the craft as a student under Farleigh in 1936, but by the mid-1950s had transferred his allegiance to painting, which remained his main creative outlet. Roderic joined the Society of Wood Engravers in 1952, but by 1965 was no longer a member, having shown just nine prints in its exhibitions between 1939 and 1960. He also exhibited prints, mainly wood engravings, with the occasional lino-cut, in his post-war solo exhibitions, as well as completing wood engravings for Christmas card and the Agricultural Contractors Limited Calendars.

The early 1950s were a high point for Roderic as a wood engraver and they saw the production of some of his most notable images in the medium. His work was getting the attention of his peers. At the Central, his brother Hugh recalled, "Farleigh said that Roderic was the best engraver he had ever known. I'm not going to disagree with that. He was superb." John Buckland Wright, the veteran printmaker and Slade School of Art teacher, author of the key 1953, volume *Etching and Engraving: Techniques and the Modern Trend*, reckoned that Barrett was "by far the most outstanding engraver of his generation, meticulous, with rare vision and invention". In a survey of the Society of Wood Engravers' first 33 years in *The Studio* magazine in 1953, that other eminent printmaker and teacher Blair Hughes-Stanton, a colleague of Barrett's at the Central, illustrating one of Roderic's prints, *Chairs and Men*, commented that it showed "not only contemporary vision but an inventiveness in technique that is only too rare."

Long after he had given up wood engraving, Roderic's prints have continued to excite enthusiasts for what Hughes-Stanton termed "one of the most beautiful of the graphic mediums." A perceptive, thoughtful appreciation of Barrett's engravings appeared in *Motif 6*, the Spring 1961 sixth edition of that short-lived but illustrious art publication. The generously illustrated article, which included two of Barrett's paintings and a whole-page reproduction of *Chairs and Men*, was by Cecil Keeling, who remarked how themes successfully employed in one medium were occasionally repeated in the other. Wood engraver Keeling explains how Roderic before engraving made "little preliminary drawing on the block itself, merely tracing down the essential lines of the design on to the surface that has been darkened with grey poster paint. He leaves little to chance, and the exact relation of the tones and the disposition of the solids are carefully assessed before he begins work with the graver. He does not, as many engravers do, take a proof of the block at several successive stages in its execution, but proofs only when the work is nearing completion."

Another perceptive admirer of Roderic's engravings is Hal Bishop, who has featured him in several exhibitions and publications, including the catalogue of *Twentieth-Century British Wood Engraving: A Celebration … and a Dissenting Voice*, his exhaustive 1997 touring exhibition. The section on Barrett is a detailed examination of his output. It ranges from the series of illustrations engraved to accompany William Cobbett's book *Rural Rides* completed by the 17-year-old Barrett at the suggestion of John Farleigh; through the last prior to war work engraving *The Blue Bird*, of 1940, "of great personal significance acknowledging the end of adolescence"; then on to the fine prints *Sleeping Chair* and *Ass and Man*, of 1950 and 1951 respectively, which "quietly demonstrate their knowledge and assimilation of the European avant-garde." Bishop believes that *Journey*, of 1951, "may be Barrett's masterpiece." In this enigmatic large print, half unengraved blackness, a naked man poles his primitive craft on a journey that is "multi-layered: light into darkness, youth into age, but always into the unknown – the human condition."

Lorna Barrett remembers a group of Shakespeare prints, including some relating to *King Lear*, dating from Roderic's studentship under Farleigh. Roderic, it seems, was not entirely satisfied with them, "but for someone who was possibly only 17 they were technically amazing, and very powerful."

Roderic eventually realised that temperamentally wood engraving, with its inability to accommodate change once the mark had been made, was not ideal for him. For someone who, after reflection, desired inordinately long periods in which to fine-tune an image, paintings in oils was the better choice. From the mid-1950s, that was his chosen medium.

John Farleigh: Melancholia
wood engraving   1935   reduced from 28 x 51cm

CHAPTER NINE

EARLY EXHIBITIONS

In 1947, the year that Barrett started to teach at the Central School, he began to prepare for his first one-man show, at The Hilton Gallery, Cambridge. This was run by Ernest Hilton, whose galleries in the city were to give Roderic several one-man exhibitions into the 1960s. Ernest's dealer son Simon, who kept in touch with Roderic after his father died, became a great enthusiast for his work, acquiring it when he could. The Hilton Gallery show was on for a few days in April and May, 1948, and comprised 40 paintings, drawings and engravings, with prices ranging from 2 guineas, for a lino-cut of *King Herod and the Cock*, to 45 guineas for the oil painting *Don Quixote and Sancho Panza VI*, given the sole black-and-white illustration in the modest catalogue. This was one of a series of pictures in various media on the *Don Quixote* theme.

It was up to Roderic to transport work to the gallery. He was a keen driver, and had earned some money driving a taxi for a Colchester firm. Cars were in short supply after the war. "I hired one, a Model T Ford, which had just two pedals, and somehow got to Cambridge and somehow got home." Barrett found The Hilton Gallery pleasant to deal with, and hoped he would show with Hilton again.

Three owners lent works to strengthen the 1948 show: Roderic's friend Charles Bonamy Dobrée, the writer and literary critic, who was for many years professor of English Literature at the University of Leeds, also Sir George Roberts and John Bullough. These early picture loans by discriminating buyers were an indication of Roderic's growing reputation as an artist, to be enhanced over the years by many mixed show appearances and the substantial list of solo exhibitions.

A surviving annotated copy of the catalogue indicates that there were sales, but Roderic was under no illusion at this stage of his career that he could live by his brush. "What one has to keep clearly in mind is that, for the first 12 years after the war, I didn't sell enough work to anywhere near cover the cost of materials, heating of the studio and so on."

In 1954, Roderic approached the Beaux Arts Gallery, in the West End of London, for a second solo show. This was a much more ambitious opening for his work, but he felt that he could approach the owner, Helen Lessore, having by this time shown work in London mixed exhibitions, at the growingly prestigious Aldeburgh Festival, elsewhere in the provinces, on the continent and having had prints acquired for the Victoria & Albert Museum collection.

At this time there were few galleries in London showing young contemporary artists. Roderic shrewdly went to the Beaux Arts, which achieved its high point in the 1950s under Mrs Lessore. It had been opened by her husband, Major Frederick Lessore, brother-in-law of the famous painter Walter Sickert, about 30 years before. When he died in 1951, she revitalised it. It soon became known for exhibiting the work of the Kitchen Sink painters, noted for their gritty urban realism. Mrs Lessore was to promote the paintings of such late twentieth century luminaries as Frank Auerbach, Francis Bacon, John Bratby, Derrick Greaves, Leon Kossoff, Edward Middleditch and Jack Smith.

Beaux Arts showed thirty paintings and four wood engravings in Roderic's 1954 solo exhibition. Again, he achieved a few sales, enough for Mrs Lessore to offer him another one-man show in 1956, but not another before the gallery closed in 1965.

Dealing with commercial galleries made Roderic realistic about the problems they faced in putting on solo shows of young artists. "It's very difficult not to have hopes, that somebody's going to say, seeing your work: 'Here's somebody worth buying.' I became rather good on the money side of showing, because when you are a failure you have a good idea of what's what. Later, I gave talks to my students, having gone around the galleries, and found about the cost of insurance, rates, rent, telephone bill and that sort of thing. One dealer had said to me: 'Never put on a one-man show of probably four or five years' work unless you are stable enough to put up with disappointment.' A gallery can't go on losing money."

Like many artists, Roderic did not find it easy to approach galleries. Lorna Barrett says: "There was this dichotomy: a tremendous belief that what he was doing was worthwhile, yet a similarly tremendous difficulty in saying to a gallery: 'This is my work, can you sell it? It is worth so many pounds.'

Yet he did persist. Barrett's next solo show in England was in 1962 at The Minories, Colchester, the first of a series through his life. The Minories was the home of the Colchester Art Society exhibitions for many years. Founded in 1946, it would become one of the most distinguished regional exhibiting societies in the country. Its Fifty Years Anniversary Exhibition, in 1996, at the nearby Chappel Galleries, was a roll-call of modern British painting, names including John Aldridge, Edward Bawden, Robert Buhler, John Nash, Kenneth Rowntree, Humphrey Spender, and Carel Weight.

Roderic's three-picture contribution to the 1962 Spring Exhibition of Colchester Art Society, made a strong impression on the critic of the *East Anglian Daily Times*, who singled it out for comment among the 90 exhibits. Barrett's big painting *Familiars* "dominates the exhibition". It was "a masterpiece. In a tightly-organised design, it links ordinary people with figures of fantasy. One woman holds a child, another a bowl of apples; a man sews on a button. With them are the mysterious presences of jesters and a grey, armed soldier, reminders of the tragedy and irony that lie behind so much of modern life."

Roderic was a founder-member, having attended the informal get-together at which the founding of a Society was first proposed. This took place in Wivenhoe, at the home of the head of Colchester School of Art, Reg Hazell. Lorna remembers the occasion when she and Roderic cycled from Frating Hall to Wivenhoe. After this exploratory meeting, local artist Henry Collins and others joined in to recruit support from Cedric Morris, co-founder of the privately run East Anglian School of Painting and Drawing, the painter John Nash and several other local luminaries to strengthen the membership. "This was the one pictorial thing that happened in Colchester, and it stayed the course," Roderic recalled in old age. "Life was so different in those pre-television days. We had two shows every year, one at the Minories and one at the Castle. I was always in favour of both. Whereas The Minories was essentially middle-class, all kinds of people went through

the Castle, it was for everybody, and it is a pity that they have not got room for us any more."

The annual meeting at The Minories was also something that eventually faded out, and the Society had the problem of finding a home for each exhibition. After John Nash died, in 1977, Morris became president and then, when he died, in 1982, Roderic succeeded him, holding the post until he died. He now had to wrestle with the ever-recurring problems of exhibition space, money and selection. "If you have an art club, then you hang everybody. If you have an art society, then it is essential that you hang works that are, in the eyes of the selection committee, sufficiently well-made to hang. Regrettably, some people must be disappointed." Roderic had a strong feeling that, as with a piece of music, prose or poetry, art must be well-crafted, and he would readily volunteer his reasons why it was or was not.

Barrett and his former Central School student Andrew Dodds met regularly at the Colchester Art Society meetings, Dodds recalls. "Because, I suppose, I have always been so indebted to him, I have always valued his opinion. If I asked him for his views, I knew his answers would be truthful, kind, wise and very sensible. There was always something quite saintly about him. And very honest."

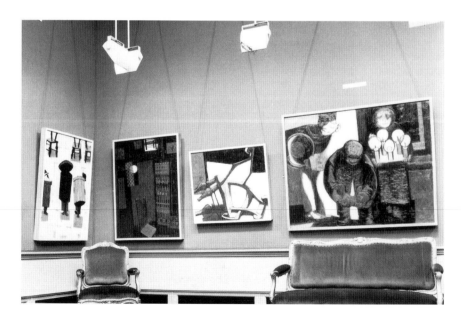

Wildenstein & Co Ltd   1961

CHAPTER TEN

IN AMERICA

Barrett was not by inclination a traveller, not surprising in someone who recalled feeling "exiled" when as a boy the family had moved for a few years from Essex to Hertfordshire. He was deeply attached to Colchester and would refer to it as "my town." He had affection for the huge old water tower, affectionately known as Jumbo, that immediately identifies the town to the incoming traveller, describing it as "a beautiful building and nobly proportioned." Lorna remembers that "if ever we were to travel, Roderic would say: 'It will take so long for my soul to catch up.'"

As the children were growing, Lorna was keen that they had foreign experience. The art of France or Italy were naturally of interest to Roderic, but he was fundamentally uneasy in strange countries, meeting new people, the food or the language. "He would become almost like a brick wall. When we went to France in a car someone had lent us and I was making for a camp site, wanting the children to get to know French children, I had to be quite sharp to persuade Roderic away from the idea of sneaking into a little wood and hiding there for a fortnight. Speaking French would be a bit daunting if you have somebody living with you who can just jabber it."

Eventually, a Barrett holiday on the continent, with a big family party staying in a villa, became a custom. Even so, Roderic's daughter Kristin agrees that "you had to use a shoehorn to get him out of Rooks End," their final home, "unless it was for tennis. He would enjoy the sights abroad, but didn't like the idea of actually going."

The Barretts' most ambitious foreign trip, to America, occurred in 1957-8. It stemmed from Lorna's family's connections there. Not only had her father moved to America to become a pastor, but before that her elder sister had married an American, who taught English at Philips Exeter Academy in New Hampshire. They owned paintings by Roderic which the art master saw, so that when he was due for a year's sabbatical, Roderic was invited during that time to take his place. "First of all, I had to go to the principal at the Central to see if he would keep my position open, as there

were not many art schools and there were an awful lot of people itching to obtain part-time teaching. William Johnstone, the principal then, was a terrible bully who, if he discovered an emotional weakness in one of his staff, he would play absolute hell with them. Although I tend to back off from rows, eventually I was pushed to have a row with him, and after that I was his golden boy. So he held my two days open while we toddled off for a year."

Although this was a dozen years after World War II had ended, life was in many ways still restricted, as was the amount of money that could be taken abroad. Roderic remembered the trip as "a bit of a lark. The ship that took Lorna and me and the three children came from Bremen and was full of immigrants, every nationality you can think of. I believe that we were the only people on board who would be coming back. The officers were German and the crew Greek, so orders would be given and not followed up because there was no common language. When we arrived in New York they were having a fight on the deck and when the chap on the dock threw a rope on board it was my son Jonathan, who was 13, who tied it up."

Kristin remembers that they were initially prevented from disembarking because it was July 4, Independence Day. "There we all were on the boat watching the fireworks, in a wonderful position by the Statue of Liberty."

Roderic had taken a lot of pictures with him, but these caused problems. While Lorna and the children left to stay with friends, Barrett was detained by Customs, who had to be assured that the pictures were by him; otherwise he would have had to pay duty on them. Roderic, who had never known such discomfort as New York in high summer, was eventually helped out, first, by a friend of the painter Keith Vaughan, with whom he had taught at the Central, who offered temporary shelter, secondly, by some pre-war Jewish friends of Lorna's. Among these was a lawyer, "who told Customs quite flatly just how little money I had with me, so I had no money to bribe them with. So they released the pictures, provided I destroyed the crates, another bit of nasty pettiness."

If Roderic had had misgivings about the trip, Philips Exeter Academy and their life there did much to reassure him that they had been right to go. The Academy, modelled on the British public school system, had a high academic standard, with tiny classes. Roderic did find the small town provincial after London, but he recalled, "quite enjoying the very intelligent bunch of boys" from wealthy homes who had qualified for entry. He was well paid for his two days a week. Part of his job was to look after the gallery belonging to the Academy, to which "some very lovely things were given."

Lorna and Kristin remember Exeter as "a wonderful place," a sharp contrast to the atmosphere of British post-war austerity which they had left behind. Barrett became very fond of his brother-in-law George Bennett, the English teacher and writer, a squash coach who shared Roderic's sporting interests. The Barretts had an enormous house and the freedom to use Academy facilities, such as the tennis court and swimming pool. For them, the wealth was astonishing. "For the first six months, it was like living in a movie," recalled Roderic. "It did the children a world of good."

Kristin remembers early family holidays at Walberswick, in Suffolk, when they would borrow a barge for a week or two from some friends. Roderic, who suffered from poor circulation, "didn't like swimming, especially in the sea, but I suppose he felt when we were younger that he had to go in with us. He used to change quickly and dive in, but gave it up as soon as we were old enough to go in by ourselves."

Cynthia Copnall remembers that Roderic "liked skimming flat stones across the sea, but loathed to swim in it. He loved to throw balls, frisbees and quoits, endearing him to the children." However, she feels that "Roderic did not really relish holidays."

Roderic's own upbringing and personality made him a liberal parent, keen to lead by example, encouraging by nature, willing to participate in the children's games, helping them to make things. He was fascinated by small children and how their minds worked, and would love to have his grandchildren and the children of visitors around him. Jonathan Barrett says: "My overall memory for us children was that he was always encouraging in whatever pursuit we undertook and, while giving gentle advice where needed, he never directed."

"I suppose Mum was more the disciplinarian," says Kristin, "which is not to say that Dad couldn't lay down the law when necessary, but there were never unnecessary rules and petty regulations. When I was very young, I had pneumonia and was not allowed up. As it was summer, every day for a while a neighbour and Dad would carry my bed outside. He would have his coffee and lunch beside me and talk about the garden and the colours, which he loved. I remember later he said: 'You know, you could never mix all the greens there are in the world.'"

The Philips Exeter Academy job also brought the bonus of a large, second-hand Studebaker, with several foils on front and dual headlights. Cars were "very, very important" to Roderic, Lorna remembers. "He never forgot that he had missed having a little toy car given to him on his eighth birthday. When we got the American car, he hated the fact that I didn't keep it clean and tidy. It meant a lot to him."

The natural co-ordination that made him a good sportsman also made him a good driver. Early on in his life, he had driven a taxi in Colchester to earn some money. When the children were growing up, Roderic would cycle three miles to Lorna's father to borrow his car to take the family out for the day. The first vehicle he owned was a Mini van. Kristin remembers how "he always wanted a sports car. When people visited with them he'd always want to sit in them. I remember thinking when he died how sad that he'd never had one, but I suppose by the time he had enough money to have bought one he felt himself too old, and he realised that family men don't have sports cars!"

The trip to America offered a unique opportunity for Roderic to extend his exhibiting outlets in a bid to launch a trans-Atlantic reputation. Unfortunate circumstances prevented his being able to take up both offers to show solo in New York. "Of galleries A and B, I chose B. One day, I loaded up the car with pictures and had the good sense to take my son Jonathan with me, because he was very good at finding his way around the place, which I wasn't. When we arrived at gallery B, we found that the directors had had a fight, and walked out! That was the end of my one-man show in New York. In retrospect, I think that the lady who offered me a show at gallery A was a better bet, anyway, but that was that."

He did, however, have two solo exhibitions during the American stay. The first was in 1957, at the Lamont Gallery, within Philips Exeter Academy, the second, in 1958, at Shore Studio Galleries, in Boston. That was very successful and might have served getting his name known across the other side of the Atlantic where New York had failed him, but again he hit Customs problems. "The gallery was in the equivalent of Bond Street, in London. I was then young, active and, having established a good relationship with Shore Galleries, the arrangement was that when I returned to England I would send paintings over. Every time that I sent them with all the proper documentation they were held by Customs. The gallery had such a bad time getting them out that eventually the arrangement was abandoned and I never sent any more."

Arrival in England after the return voyage left indelible impressions on Roderic's memory. "When I saw the enormous bobby on the dock at Liverpool, with a spike on his helmet, it's a funny thing to say, but I could have hugged him, because he hadn't got a gun. On the train journey back, to London and then on to Colchester, there was the feeling that there wasn't a hedge or a ditch or a piece of land that hadn't been looked after and cultivated for donkeys' years, a contrast to Exeter, where the land was poor."

The Barretts arrived back in England "with a pocketful of money and well-clothed, although we had to pay income tax in England as well as in America". As well as Roderic having made a few hundred pounds from his salary at the American Academy, the Barretts had been able to rent out their house in Colchester. They had lived there from 1947. Lorna remembers it as "a delightful little house, built exactly on the pattern of Roderic's father's, a matter of Barrett pride, I think, but it wasn't right for us.

The design was odd, the orientation was wrong and the pitch of the roof made it terribly inefficient in terms of space and cost, and it was cold."

The energetic Cecil Barrett had continued with his house building in Colchester. He was to keep active until, in old age, he fell and broke his hip. It distressed Roderic to see his father pathetically unable to walk properly again. (Plate 116)

In 1959, the year after their return to England, the Barretts moved to Rooks End, Stanway, outside Colchester. Lorna would have preferred to stay in the town. Mark now no longer had the companionship of his older brother and sister who had left home. He was attending the Grammar School in the town and welcomed having friends close by. However, Roderic had been hankering to live more in the country. He found it difficult to have near neighbours and on occasions felt hemmed in.

Another practical reason for moving was that as Roderic painted the pictures were building up, and storage space was needed. The relocation to Rooks End would provide this as well as privacy, an extensive garden and his specially made shed studio, brought with them from Prettygate Road, where Roderic would be able to work until he died. (left)

A field and Stanway Church separated Rooks End from the busy A12 road. The house was not purpose-built but a conversion of attractive stables, with accommodation above. In its final configuration, over the many years the Barretts were there it retained its singular disposition of rooms and unique atmosphere.

For many of the years that they had lived in Colchester, in early spring Roderic would have to take to his bed for several days as the stress of teaching weighed on him, clearly a psychosomatic illness. "He wasn't skiving, would have sweats at night and looked really ill in the morning," Lorna remembers. "If he was ill on Wednesday and Thursday, when he taught, we would have to get a chit from the doctor. Technically, you couldn't, as you had to be ill for three days to qualify for National Insurance. But we had an understanding doctor who would give us one, as he rightly argued that Roderic was earning all his week's money on just those two days."

"Roderic was a very fragile person, depressed when he couldn't work, and the world could be frightening for him. After we were settled at Rooks End the depressions suffered from annually diminished. Less people around Roderic helped, I think."

CHAPTER ELEVEN

ROYAL ACADEMY SCHOOLS

Roderic resumed his teaching at the Central School two days, including evenings, a week. He would cycle to the station in Colchester on Wednesday and return on Thursday, staying overnight in London with the artist Hugh Mackinnon and his family to reduce travelling, as the train journey each way took an hour and three quarters. Hugh is remembered by the Barretts as perceptive and intelligent. He and his family were always great friends, and Roderic blessed this broadening influence. Mackinnon was for a time on the staff of the Central and also taught for many years at Hornsey College of Art.

Roderic became increasingly dissatisfied with the staffing situation at the Central and began to look for another job. "This was not easy, but I thought I would start at the top and work down." Interviews at the Slade School of Fine Art and St Martin's School of Art did not lead to anything, so Roderic next approached Peter Greenham, keeper at the Royal Academy Schools – effectively, their director – who had been appointed in 1964 to the post which he was to occupy until 1985. A diffident, retiring man, Greenham ran the Schools in an enlightened and informal manner and was greatly admired by his pupils.

Greenham could offer Roderic just one day a week. For a time, he combined this with his regular two days weekly at the Central, until eventually he had to tell Greenham that the burden was too much and the single Royal Academy day would have to be forfeited. "It didn't have to do with time and pursuing my own work, but with some sort of frailty in myself in that I could not cope with teaching that amount. It is hard to explain, as I loved teaching.

"I was loath to give up the Academy, as I knew that I could be happy there, but by the time Saturday morning came I was whacked. I was resigned to returning to teaching only at the Central. Then, in the nick of time, I got the offer of another day at the Academy Schools, and Greenham made up the money so that I got the same amount as I got at the Central."

Having made his arrangement with Greenham to teach again for only two days a week on Wednesdays and Thursdays, the pressure was off him and Roderic had more time for his own work.

Roderic was to stay at the Schools from 1968 to 1996, and always got on well with Greenham who was, like him, a serious painter. "I was the only member of staff teaching two days a week, and I was left alone. The only thing I was asked to do was to write a report at the end of the year on all the students." At Rooks End, his own painting continued. Lorna remembers: "After teaching on Wednesdays and Thursdays he was very, very tired and in term time it would be difficult for him to paint, but on Saturday mornings he certainly worked."

An august institution, the RA Schools, housed in daunting subterranean, cast-littered corridors, stemmed from the 1768 Instrument of Foundation of the Royal Academy of Arts. The Schools enjoyed a high reputation in the first half of the nineteenth century, but had come in for criticism in the second half. In the first half of the twentieth century, the Royal College of Art, particularly under the charismatic leadership of William Rothenstein, and the relatively new Slade School of Fine Art, where students could study under such luminaries as Henry Tonks and Philip Wilson Steer, continued to challenge the Royal Academy Schools' ability to attract the best talent, although by the time that Roderic arrived they were beginning again to be highly regarded. His contribution did much to enhance that reputation.

"It was a privileged situation," Roderic recalled after he left. "There were only about 40 or 50 painting students, all postgraduates, there for three years. When I had studied at the Central, I had three years in total. At the Royal Academy Schools a student would have had a foundation year somewhere, then three years somewhere else and then a further three at the Schools, if they got in, seven years in all. Although attendance there, like attendance at the Royal College, gave a certain amount of prestige, it guaranteed no work at the end. What it did offer was a wonderful place to work: a live model every day, a wonderful collection of plaster casts and quite good studios. (below/overleaf: Roderic in the Schools)

"The Schools had a very nice atmosphere, and I was happy there for many years. We never had a staff meeting. Greenham said that, before I arrived, 'we did have one, but I decided that it was so acrimonious that we wouldn't have any others!' Greenham was a law unto himself. He wouldn't have many RAs on his staff, I can tell you."

Not surprisingly, Roderic eyed with a droll scepticism what is an essentially Establishment institution. When he joined the staff, Roderic recalled a strong ex-Royal College of Art lobby active when it came to electing Academicians. Although he accepted that some RAs were good painters, "some are very poor ones." He was for quite a while a candidate to be elected, with strong backers, but eventually withdrew his name after being time and again rejected. Later, he agreed that the right as an RA of being able to hang six pictures in the annual Summer Exhibition would have been useful to him, but as he claimed to complete only about two a year he would have been unlikely to take full advantage of this.

Two things, Roderic claimed, prompted him to withdraw his name. First, "I fell out with Sir Roger de Grey," from 1984–93 Royal Academy president, over judgement of work. "I am not very good at saying flattering things about people's paintings. It is not one of my gifts." The other reason for withdrawal was "the huge, very posh dinner, with royalty present, each year at the time of the Summer Exhibition. One year I went, begging and borrowing a pair of trousers, a jacket and a bow tie for the occasion. Your name is shouted out and you shake hands with the president and vice-president, you have drinks and, on the day that I went, they had six guardsmen in busbies with silver trumpets to announce the royal visitors, then we all trooped in. I was ashamed to be there. I asked myself, what had such a snobbish occasion got to do with art?"

His brother Hugh, who lent Roderic shoes for that annual dinner, recalled another occasion when Roderic had encountered royalty. "Bet you don't know who I've been hobnobbing with? – the Prince of Wales!" He had come to look at students' work and Roderic had been delegated to escort Prince Charles and his detective for three quarters of an hour. "Roderic was so amused. He hadn't even got a tie on, being dressed as he always was for teaching."

For Roderic all of this was a side issue compared to his relationship with his students and a few members of staff. As at the Central, he found this metropolitan teaching stimulating and invigorating, an inspiration to do his own work. We get a flavour of Roderic as teacher at the Schools from the memories of Ron Sims and Robin Warnes, who were both his students,

Sims during Barrett's earliest days there, 1967–70, Warnes about a decade later when Roderic was well established.

Sims "appeared to be an ideal student for Roderic, coming from Essex and shape-obsessed. He would continually question my shape relationships and their position to the picture edge. I realised that there was an empathy between us, partly because of the way he worked his own compositions with abstract shapes as a platform to let figurative images float on top. Although my own work has always been abstract, Roderic was quite excited one day at the RA Schools when I experimented with some strange figurative cartoon imagery."

After his time at the Schools, Sims and Roderic would meet at Colchester Art Society meetings, lectures, private views such as those at the Chappel Galleries and at home. "Often we chatted about life, career prospects and how to survive in cold outdoor wooden-built studios in Essex: lots of discussions about different forms of heating and how many pairs of socks were needed in our boots to combat icy conditions. This seemed to parallel the number of works we could produce of the four-foot size approximately in any one year. I think 12 large paintings was the target, although invariably we produced less.

"He was always thoughtful when coming across any problems in meetings, and able to make a succinct, meaningful comment, generally laced with dry humour and wit, with a mischievous twinkle in his eye. Most art work to Roderic was either good or bad, although I managed to confuse him once with one of my pictures which had a pink abstract sun image in a predominantly green and yellow painting. He repeatedly covered the pink image with his hand in an attempt to come to a thoughtful decision."

Warnes, who like Sims knew Barrett over a long period, came to respect him "as an artist and as man. I first met Roderic in 1977 when he was interviewing students who had applied to the RA Schools. From our first meeting I realised that he was a person with high standards, with little compromise.

"In my last year at the Schools, Roderic was my tutor. His great ability as a teacher was that he could work with the individual. I can remember him saying to me: 'Have you seen my book?'. I replied 'No,' so we sat in the corridor in the Schools and Roderic then produced this book with wonderful illustrations of various artists from Titian to Mondrian. There was no escape with Roderic when he was teaching the visual language. This

was one of his strengths: an ability to convey the essentials of what makes good art, not the trimmings. This, in my opinion, is what made him an excellent teacher and painter. He would make you look at the work rather than the image.

"Roderic could be quite scary, because he made you think about your work. Later, when I had one-man shows, I was always anxious about Roderic turning up, because you knew that he had the ability to find something that you hadn't noticed before, which you accepted and loved him for. He had the incredible ability to understand what a student was doing."

Until Roderic's death, he and Warnes would share studio visits to compare notes on their work and art in general. "There was still no compromise. You had to come up with the goods. He would send me notes on the back of envelopes, such as, 'Firm suggestion to you: do have at least five works on the go, so that there is almost certain to be one that you can really attack. It is a way to avoid that "What shall I do today?" feeling. There you are, then!'"

CHAPTER TWELVE

THE BUSY EXHIBITOR

Roderic was always giving students such as Sims and Warnes a practical demonstration of how to do it by regularly exhibiting his own work. As well as showing widely in group exhibitions in London, the provinces and abroad, solo exhibitions in Britain and the provinces continued in his middle years.

After his 1962 solo show at The Minories, Roderic kept up a busy exhibiting schedule until the end of his life. There was a show shared with Hugh Mackinnon in 1964 at the Holland Park Gallery in London; a series of one-mans including several at the Alwin Gallery from 1966; two at the Oxford Gallery and one at the Playhouse Gallery, Harlow, in the first half of the 1970s; and in the 1970s and 1980s solo exhibitions at the Universities of Southampton, Warwick and Keele and at the Thackeray Gallery, London; with a return to Harlow in 1984. These attracted encouraging press notices, where the unusual quality of his symbolism did not pass unnoticed. There were always critics ready to offer an interpretation, if often somewhat tentative.

The Alwin Gallery, in Mayfair, was an interesting venue that mixed a range of two- and three-dimensional talents. In the catalogue foreword to Roderic's second exhibition there, in 1967, Anthony Day did not attempt to interpret Barrett's symbolism. He was content with the judgement that his pictures belonged "less to the art of their time than to the life of their time … a humanist, committed to the abiding theme of human adversity." Barrett had concentrated his meaning "into images of powerful simplicity … imbued with pity and understanding." (overleaf: studio shot for Alwin Gallery poster)

A time for reflection on what Barrett had accomplished so far was the sizeable retrospective that took place at The Minories, Colchester, in 1973, a slight variation on which toured to Castle Museum, Norwich, in 1974. In its rather larger Minories version, this comprised 95 works in all: 61 oil paintings, 28 drawings and six prints, quite a few retrieved for the occasion from private collections.

The perceptive foreword was by Roderic's friend Alex Comfort, the polymath physician, poet, novelist and writer on anarchy. The author of many books, including essays gathered together in *Art and Social Responsibility*, 1947, he was to become world-famous in the year of Roderic's Minories show when his best-seller *The Joy of Sex* appeared. Roderic and Lorna Barrett's friendship with Comfort extended back to the wartime years at the Frating community, where he lived for a while. Comfort, too, was a conscientious objector. The three were to keep in touch, Alex visiting them at Rooks End and his first wife, Ruth, also visiting if passing their way.

After examining the iconography of the pictures at The Minories and the Castle Museum, "highly individual but difficult to describe", Comfort concluded that Roderic was an "original artist, whose work has undoubtedly suffered in exposure because of its scale – all of the most impressive canvases are large, and involve a use of large fields of colour which are simply not reducible." Although Barrett had by then had prints acquired by the Victoria & Albert Museum, and would contribute to the Universities of Essex and Southampton and several provincial collections, Comfort's mid-career comment that "the amount of his work in public galleries bears no relation to his originality and importance as a painter" was to apply throughout his life, and does still.

Comfort reckoned the 1973–74 retrospective "a major event. Our culture finds the subject-matter which is highly disturbing at the unconscious level, easier to take in drama than in visualisation: there is a sense in which Barrett is the artistic counterpart of Beckett and Pinter in the sources of unease which he generates, the same unease which many people experience in the presence of dolls. An assemblage of his painting is an artistically rewarding but profoundly disquieting experience, antidotal in insight to the shallow media image of 'togetherness' and domesticity, but none the less salutary for that, in revealing the poverty which underlies superficial prosperity, and the unspoken rituals and characters which underlie our home lives, emerging only in dreams, in depressive illness, or in the vision of a talented artist such as this."

In his *Arts Review* write-up on Barrett's 1978 exhibition at the Thackeray Gallery in London, Richard Walker reckoned the painter's imagery "closest to the Flemish Belgians – Permeke, Ensor, 'Peasant' Bruegel – but his feeling, unlike theirs, is always affirmative, life-giving, precisely because existence here has been rendered down into a vocabulary of formal relations and realised as a visual unity above all." For Walker, "form was the means of expressing life, space and time. Form, by its very nature, solid, enduring, actual. These were the thoughts that Barrett's feelings gave rise to. The *feelings* they gave rise to are a calmness emanating from the formal solidity".

Hugh Barrett remembered that Roderic "always said he didn't embark upon a painting until he had had at least two years thinking about

it". Getting the form right was clearly crucial to Barrett and the indications are that the images chosen were not importantly bowls, hoops, skulls, and so on, but essential shapes, the symbolism often being subconscious. Roderic's daughter Kristin supposes that "a lot of his demons were there and needed to come out, and they came out in certain ways. But they all had a sense of order. Where things were placed, balanced by shadows, where lines were, he could explain all that. Ideally, he would have lived in a tidy house. He didn't, but his studio was tidy. Even if there were dirty rags, they would be in a box or something. He did like order in his life."

Lorna agrees that the objects in pictures were at times "quite accidental. He just wanted a dot here or a bit of something there, but occasionally they were very meaningful to him. Roderic used a limited number of objects and knew them inside-out. He was largely unconscious about what he was saying with the candles and other things. There are some fairly explicit ones, like the woman with scissors and a candle," a theme of several pictures. Mark remembers that Roderic did not like to explain what his paintings were about, he was primarily concerned with the painting itself – design, form, balance – and not any external meaning of its contents.

Roderic clearly thought highly of Alex Comfort's assessment of his work because, after his contribution to the 1973 retrospective, another that had appeared some years before was used for the catalogue of the 1984 show that toured from The Minories to The Playhouse, Harlow. Having alluded to the French playwright Jean Anhouilh's description of the dinner-table as a microcosm of society, Comfort found in Barrett's work "something more disturbing, a microcosm of the themes of tragedy and the unconscious…." His "private but very hard-hitting iconography makes him a disturbing painter, projecting into domestic scenes and objects the entire subconscious jungle which underlies them". However, Comfort detected "little of the sense of menace which the schizophrenic sees in his environment", everything being "controlled by his sense of scale and composition, so that it acquires the formal dignity of tragedy".

After studying with Roderic during his early years at the RA Schools, Ron Sims remained intrigued by his images and what they suggest. As an astute practitioner, he realised that his old teacher's canvases were essentially "cleverly designed in what are basically abstract compositions." He feels that Barrett lost by being stylistically associated with the Kitchen

Sink painters of the 1950s. Rather, "he should have been somewhere in the Ken Kiff range in recent contemporary trends where strange or mythical imagery is explored. I think one could then reach back to Blake, Fuseli, Goya and Bosch – all artists with heightened personal imagination."

Barrett's eldest son Jonathan had gone on to train as an architect. "After finishing my training I used to occasionally meet my father at the Royal Academy for lunch. We would discuss issues such as the importance of corners on a building, building rhythm and doorways. He always had insights into our physical surroundings that came from a well-trained eye." When Jonathan was still a child, the aesthetically fastidious Roderic had commented of his work: "I don't know how he places objects and people as well as he does. His sense of design is impeccable."

Jonathan also recalls "as a child the excitement in our house when my father's studio arrived on the back of a truck. The studio had been constructed in Suffolk by a friend of Roderic's brother, Hugh. It settled at the bottom of the garden. I have memories of visiting it, the smell of oil paint and the precious times when we children were encouraged to come and paint." Another of his memories is of "being sat on a child's seat on the cross-bar of my father's bicycle. The purpose of one journey was going to Olivers Woods where he did some drawings. Of particular note was seeing my first Kingfisher beside the small river there."

Although the pre-fabricated wooden studio remained in use for decades, in many ways it was not ideal. Vivienne Loomes, visiting Barrett on the occasion of his 1973 Minories show, wrote that "he admits to a running battle there with mice, although you suspect that he has a soft spot for them really, simply because he is that sort of man."

One of Roderic's pleasures at the RA Schools was a weekly lunch with his printmaker colleague Peter Freeth, who remembers that "we laughed a lot of the time, but were very serious about it. Politically, in the widest possible sense, we faced the same direction and groaned in harmony. He seemed to me to come from somewhere deep in English history, from many places, indeed. It is easy to see him with the Diggers or Levellers, at the Putney debates, with Tom Paine, Cobbett, Hogarth, Blake, Gillray, with all those passionate Non-Conformists, protestants, radicals, with the men of Essex in all those marches on the capital. He reminded me, too, of the 'village – Hampden, that with dauntless breast' of Gray's *Elegy*.

"And yet, with his doubts – his passionate doubts – he was also a thoroughly modern man. Naturally on the left, the sceptic in him made him suspicious of any Cause. No New Model Army would have fully satisfied Roderic, or New World Colony long detained him. His glass was always half full – but those who knew it was half empty could, perhaps, just have a point…. He was wise enough to know he might be wrong, and generous enough to concede that the other man might be right … probably was right, in fact.

"He remained blessedly young at heart (and enviably sprightly in body) and enjoyed teaching because he loved being with young people. Young people, young artists, are dreamers like him, with their freshness and hope, their uncertainties and vulnerability, not touched by cynicism and compromise….. A lovely man, good friend, great spirit."

(below from left: Lorna, Roderic at the Holland Park Gallery 1964; Hugh Barrett and Lorna at the Alwin Gallery 1966; Roderic with co-exhibitors, Playhouse Gallery, Harlow 1977)

CHAPTER THIRTEEN

ARTISTS AT WORK

Meanwhile, Roderic continued with his teaching at the RA Schools. This was on a one-to-one basis, which he favoured. He continued to win the admiration and affection of many of the younger students, as he had his earlier ones, such as Sims and Warnes.

Susan-Jayne Hocking and Rachel Widdows were postgraduate students of Roderic's. Susan-Jayne, at the Schools from 1987–90, writes that her "memories of 'Uncle Rodders', as we used to call him, are very fond indeed. He was a lovely kind, gentle man. Out of all our tutors at the Royal Academy, he was the one who gave himself wholeheartedly to the students and their work. It was not just a job, it was a passion to help young artists open their minds to the endless possibilities for their creativity. He was a rare artist who could articulate about painting without all the bullshit. Many students felt it was very unfair that he was not made a Royal Academician. I think he was very underrated as an artist at the Academy.

"My lasting memory of Uncle Rodders is from a tutorial. If he didn't like something in a painting you were working on, or he believed it just didn't work, he would say: 'You couldn't sell me that bit of painting, not even on a very dark night!' He was never rude or hurtful in his criticism, just honest in his belief. And he was always right."

Rachel Widdows remembers Barrett's "not even on a very dark night" quip and also believes that "he was clearly underrated by the RA, who should have made him a Royal Academician." She "met Roderic in 1989 when I began my MA and he became my personal tutor. He dispensed pearls of wisdom with honesty and humour, using strongly visual language that became famous as Rodericisms, such as describing a particularly ill-conceived, negative space as a 'soft slug'. I owe my sensitivity to construction and composition to his kindly interventions. At times he could be very straight-talking, but underlying his words was a passionate artist who genuinely wanted to help. I, like many of the students, appreciated and needed his honesty and lack of pretension. He stood out among his peers by refusing to make compromises just to fit into the commercial art world."

In addition to his regular teaching, Barrett explained how he would give his two talks. "There was the one on the business of money, how to approach galleries and how not to, being courteous, making appointments and so on, which the young do not always think about, and another on the basics of visual language."

Visual language formed a chapter in Roderic's privately published, illustrated book *Artists at Work*, which appeared in 1999, edited and produced by his son Mark. It is the distillation of a lifetime spent involved in practising, teaching, reading about, looking at and, above all, thinking about painting and all aspects of the visual arts. The commentary is by Barrett, illuminated by numerous quotations on aspects of the arts by practitioners as diverse as Dante, Housman, Mondrian, Pasternak, Proust and Stravinsky. These had been collected over many years, kept in a card index and eventually typed out by Lorna when the book came to be compiled.

Verbally, Barrett was most articulate, but he was not naturally equipped to be a writer. Lorna remembers that he was well read and he loved poetry for which, like music, he had a real feeling and of which he wrote a fair amount. "Auden was a very big person for him. They were broadly contemporary, of course, and they had gone down the same road politically."

When it came to the compilation, Mark had quite a few problems to surmount, as he edited the text and typed it into the computer. "Although he read widely, loved poetry and was articulate, his written language was not always grammatically correct," says his son, who eventually had the task of ironing out the various anomalies. "His writing was original but idiosyncratic; if you had sentences without a verb, he didn't see why you should do anything about it – and as long as the meaning was clear, why should you?," Mark and Roderic butted heads over the preponderance of quotations. "The original text was more than half quotes, so all the time I was saying: 'Dad, we want to hear what *you've* got to say, with a seasoning of quotes, not an anthology of them. There are hundreds of those about.'"

Artists at Work stemmed from its author's "wish to share my excitement at the intelligent and sensitive thoughts others have had," coupled with the illuminating thoughts of a serious and lifelong practitioner, which should have a much wider circulation. It was Barrett's "attempt to quote and say the obvious about the artist's emotional and practical problems: an attempt to write out those factors which are in some way consistent, though the effect any one of them has on an individual because of what he is and when and where he lives, may be very different."

Barrett is modest about his own contributions to the book, which are "mainly concerned with writing about some of the obvious elements that are common to all the visual arts." These range over such subjects as Weight, Proportion, Habits of Work, Judgement and Style. He emphasises that "paintings are physical things and we responding physical bodies. And that through our senses we can be profoundly moved."

The book which Ron Sims had earlier been privileged to see during its gestation, was much later still a sort of unseen Holy Grail to students at the Schools. Rachel Widdows recalls "a rumour that Roderic had written a book full of idiosyncratic words of wisdom. It was a source of endless speculation, with some of the students even claiming to have read it. It is a measure of Roderic's status that the contents were debated without the book ever being seen. Many years later at an exhibition of Roderic's I told him about these rumours and he amazed me by admitting that there was a book, but that he had no recollection of ever showing it to any students. I was delighted and honoured to receive a copy of his Artists' Bible, as I call it, shortly afterwards. This book brought me much closer to knowing Roderic. I realised just what an uncompromisingly honest, deep thinker he had been. The book is full of wonderful, helpful guidance for the working artist, written in his own voice – passionate, truthful, and thoughtful but accessible."

Anyone who met Barrett for the first time in his later years encountered not an old man but someone still full of a boyish zeal. This infects the Introduction of *Artists at Work*, where the discovery of a quotation such as Debussy's that "Music is the space between the notes" leaves him "wanting to shout into the air." He recognises that among the quotations included will be some that are paradoxical and contradictory, yet contends that "though two comments may come from opposite directions,

both may clarify." The quotations, which for him remained "rewarding and cheering however often I read them," were an assurance that "there is no need to be alone."

Alongside his quotation-compiling, RA Schools work and other commitments, Roderic kept up his group exhibition and solo show commitments through the late 1980s and early 1990s. There were a couple of Suffolk shows, one in 1987 at Christchurch Mansion, in Ipswich; another in 1988 at the Phoenix Gallery, Lavenham, a private gallery with a strong record of promoting East Anglian artists; and a third, in Essex, in 1990, at the Beecroft Gallery at Westcliff-on-Sea. In a lengthy *Arts Review* appreciation published a few days before the Phoenix Gallery show opened, Ray Rushton found Barrett "one of the most significant painters in East Anglia, arguably in the country.… Here is a man who loves people and recognises that he is at one with their condition."

His first solo exhibition at the Chappel Galleries, near Colchester, in 1993, excited much interest and some informed printed comment. Writing a foreword for the exhibition card, Sister Wendy Beckett found that "a true artist is alive and well and living in Essex. Roderic Barrett creates work that satisfies all our human needs as art-lovers." As well as his response to beauty, he "shows us the sadness at the heart of things." Beckett realised that it was "never safe to embark too confidently on explanations of a work by Barrett. The subtleties and multiple significances can make a commentary seem trivial." She found in "these majestic paintings … a visual image, never a verbal one."

Beckett reckoned Barrett's still life pictures his most beautiful, in which she saw "his immense graphic power in all its strength." Writing in the regional arts magazine *Images*, Verity Wookey drew attention to the "sense of mystery" which the still lifes shared with their "players on the stage of life" counterparts, as well as a humorous aspect. "He invests his simple objects with nobility and stillness, while conveying his affection for them, and sometimes the hint of a quiet chuckle." As a painter, Wookey drew attention to crucial placing of all components in Barrett's pictures and "the great beauty of surface and richness of colour" of his canvases.

Barrett continued teaching well beyond the normal retirement age, but eventually began to reduce his commitment. In later life Roderic was delighted to meet so many students "who were making a living at their painting, which is something I was never able to do." He was open-minded as he had been at the Central, recalling without criticism one Central School student "whose canvas had a hole in it from which lumps of coal appeared." An example of his willingness to embrace was his attendance at the Saatchi Collection-related Sensation exhibition at the Royal Academy in 1997. "The thing that I was good at was that I could interest myself in what anybody was doing. I was prepared to look at it and discuss it. In the end, it all comes down to relationships between factors on a canvas, whether it is paint or lumps of wood.

"But eventually I thought, my goodness, I'm tired. I don't want to do two days a week any more. I thought that the RA Schools would say: 'All right, then, you'd better leave altogether!' But I have often been extremely lucky, and they let me do just the one day. That continued for several years, and then it crept up on me that I could no longer be bothered with lumps of coal coming through a canvas." Barrett retired from teaching in 1996 when he "still had a whack of energy left, for a short run," to devote to his own work. Leonard McComb, then RA Schools keeper, did offer Roderic four days a term to retain his services, but he felt that he would be no longer sufficiently in touch with the students.

Barrett could be droll about the business of teaching. The self-taught painter Waj Mirecki recalls how he was requested, for the first time, to address a watercolour workshop in France. So he asked Barrett, with his vast experience, how he would go about it. "Simple. Just give them lots of paradoxical and contradictory advice and you're home and dry," was the reply, says Mirecki. After this advice was recounted to the artist Josef Herman, "he knitted his brow, nodded sagely and said: 'What a very wise man.'"

Sister Wendy Beckett with Roderic Barrett discussing his painting *Them and Us* on the programme 'Moving Art' Anglia TV 1991

CHAPTER FOURTEEN

RETIREMENT YEARS

Barrett had plenty to do during his few retirement years. There was the regular painting schedule, preparing for exhibitions such as his own and, as its president, those of Colchester Art Society, work towards his book, his tennis and visits from his grandchildren and great-grandchildren, a particular delight. "He took pride in and gained joy from his family," recalls his RA Schools colleague, and fellow-luncher Peter Freeth. "I never witnessed it myself, but can imagine him in his garden rambling with the little ones to their mutual delight.

"Never wait for the spirit to move you," was Barrett's disciplined attitude to painting. Lorna remembers that "he was very strict about going into the studio shed, and for years it was a real shed, at about nine o'clock in the morning until lunch time. After a bit of time off then, he would work as long as he could in the afternoon." Barrett told one interviewer: "I paint only in natural light, not only because I hate painting in artificial light, but also to restrict the amount of work I would do."

When he had started painting many years before, he would have only one picture on the easel, which he would gradually try to resolve. Then he discovered, replicating his advice to his RA Schools pupil Robin Warnes, "that if I had about six on the go and painted them in rotation, I could spend one day on each. At the end of the day, I would turn a picture's face to the wall until next week, so that I had the maximum surprise when I turned it round. One of the problems with painting, especially if you take a long time, is that you get accustomed to what is there, and that is fatal. You must look at it as if it is by somebody else, seeking errors."

One who remembers with affection regular visits to Rooks End is the painter Charles Debenham, Colchester Art Society chairman from 1974–90. For him, Roderic was inseparable from "his studio shed and the little dog." Roderic and Lorna owned two female north border terriers, one after the other, called Jenny and Jesse. After Roderic's death Charles found "a reminder of our last 'analysing session' in his studio. These 'sessions' meant putting my latest work in a cardboard box and taking it together with a bottle of wine to Rooks End. Going into the studio with all his paintings faced to the wall, I was given a chair and a corkscrew. Roderic put my first offering on his easel and after a long silence, the analysis began. Halfway down the bottle it was my turn to bat, but by then our appreciation of art was much more direct and the problems much easier to solve. I always came away a little richer and now when I believe I've finished a picture I stop and think 'Ah! yes – but what would Roderic say?'"

The frequently sombre tone of Barrett's pictures is one aspect of his work that not infrequently comes in for comment. Debenham remembers saying on one occasion: "Roderic, there must be *some* bright colours!" In the mid-1970s, Roderic was operated on for cataracts by the London eye surgeon John Dobree. Cataracts were a family problem with the Barretts and his brothers also underwent the operation. For a painter, it was a traumatic experience. Mark feels that there was a benefit, that there was "a greater effluence of colour" and that his father's pictures "livened up" after the cataracts were removed.

"Some paintings would go on for years and years and years," remembers Barrett's daughter Kristin. "Somebody else might consider it finished, but something would bother him, maybe the colour or placing of an object. It might be a big change or so small that another person wouldn't notice it, then he would change it again. Occasionally, paintings that had been sold would come back to be revarnished, and he'd ask the owner: 'Do you mind if I redo this bit?' He found it very hard to actually say that a painting was finished. Around him in his studio would be his props, the objects which helped him: bowls, skulls of which he had lots, baskets, a chair, his dad's hat, and so on." Then there were the omnipresent candles, of course, which his brother Hugh, so close to him for many years, recalled "mean time, Roderic was quite emphatic about that."

Another person who was surprised by the long gestation of

pictures, was the writer from the *Essex County Standard* who interviewed Roderic on the occasion of his Chappel Galleries 80th Anniversary show in 2000. The article explained that it was often difficult to date one of Roderic's paintings because of their long duration. "I've got one that certainly covers 40 years." Rather than finding this constant dissatisfaction a curse, Barrett found it a blessing. "Being blind, or not knowing what to do, that's hell, but if you can see what you should do, that's wonderful…. You have to be very grateful if you can see what should be done."

Barrett is unusual among English painters because of the lack of landscape in his work, remaining essentially a painter of objects and figures. He did produce a few abstracts and exhibited them, reckoning that they included some of his best works. He once completed a large panel for some Dutch friends, who requested it after they had moved to an architect-designed house in the Colchester area, but temperamentally he disliked painting to order. Kristin remembers that when they were in America, her father was asked to paint a memorial portrait of some acquaintances' daughter who had died young. Roderic agonised over it, then said: "I just can't do it. I wouldn't do it justice," and it was never attempted.

Roderic was past his mid-seventies when he retired from teaching, but retained the vigour and alertness of a much younger man. However, Kristin remembers visiting him latterly and receiving his comment that when that day he had looked in the mirror "I was horrified to see the face of an old man, whereas I feel so young inside."

Sociable but not gregarious would probably sum up Barrett's attitude to people. His brother Hugh believed that Roderic missed the company of like-minded painters and students at the RA Schools after retirement. The close relationship that Roderic and his slightly older brother Hugh had had as small boys was replicated during the last 30 years of their lives. Hugh, who died within months of Roderic, recalled that latterly they were "as close as two people can be".

Barrett would always make time for those he liked who visited Rooks End and on occasions welcomed such ex-students as Susan-Jayne Hocking, Rachel Widdows and Andrew Gadd, a figurative painter with whom he empathised. Susan-Jayne remembers: "Rachel and I went to visit Uncle Rodders at his lovely home and gave him a tutorial in his studio to repay him for all his hours of dedication to us. We had lunch, spent many hours looking over his work and came to the conclusion that his best was

always hidden away in a corner, not the paintings he was showing at the RA Summer Exhibition. He was never a commercial artist in his head and his work portrays this freedom. I believe he painted very much for himself and not for applause."

Rachel recalls the visit and that "he was working on a large painting showing various characters standing on a stage, one with an umbrella. I don't know what advice we gave, but I don't suppose it was especially helpful. The studio was immaculate, with every brush cleaned and palette spotless. Roderic coined one of his classic comments, when he explained why so many of his canvases were turned to the wall, saying: 'I will not be bullied by my paintings,' a sentiment that many painters are sure to recognise."

Even if Roderic would accommodate the occasional visitor Kristin, who would call in to see him frequently after teaching, delighting him with stories of the children, says that "it was always made very clear, certainly to us as children and to others that when he was working he was working, and just because he was doing it at home it didn't mean you could drop in willy-nilly. The only thing that interfered was tennis. Tennis was sacrosanct." Twice a week in the afternoons, he played with friends. Roderic had been athletic at school, a keen soccer player and continued with his tennis until his last winter, as Lorna says, leaping around "like a ping-pong ball on the court."

Roderic continued just after he finished teaching to show at the Royal Academy Summer Exhibition. His brother Oliver O'Connor had first shown two wood carvings there in 1933. Because of his long absence in America, Connor was to exhibit only twice more, a wood carving in 1975 and a bronze in 1983, whereas Roderic, who made his first appearance in 1970, between then and 1997, his final year, steadily showed at Burlington House, in all 51 pictures.

Just before retirement, Roderic had a solo exhibition at the European Parliament's Assembly Rooms, in Strasbourg, France, which Roderic, Lorna and her brother Frank attended. This had an interesting gestation. Anne McIntosh, then Member of that Parliament for Essex North and Suffolk South and later Member of Parliament for the Vale of York, had been so impressed by Barrett's exhibition, organised by Edna and Waj Mirecki at Chappel Galleries in 1993, that she initiated the Strasbourg show. Chappel Galleries then took over, handling the complicated financial, transport and bi-lingual publicity and exhibition literature. They had valuable support from Essex County Council and from Michael Chase the former director of The Minories in Colchester, husband of the artist Valerie Thornton. Both were friends and patrons of Roderic's. The Mireckis had for some years known the British Ambassador in Luxembourg, Nick Elam. He was notified of the Strasbourg show, lunched with Roderic and the Mireckis in Strasbourg and agreed to display pictures in his official residence in Luxembourg after the exhibition was over, which Chappel Galleries arranged. Elam was then hosting the prestigious Churchill Memorial Lectures.

When Barrett's next big solo exhibition took place, his 1996 retrospective at the Concourse Gallery at the Barbican Art Centre, in London, followed by a showing at firstsite, The Minories, Elam recalled his early acquaintanceship with the artist's work as a Colchester schoolboy in the 1950s. "I found it haunting. My mother found it haunting. She would talk about the dangerous-looking children. I would think about the dangerous-looking furniture. These images, and our shared reactions, stayed with me vividly."

The well-illustrated catalogue remains a fine record of Barrett's work. There were perceptive essays by Professor Thomas Puttfarken, of the University of Essex's Department of Art History and Theory, and the critic Andrew Patrizio. Puttfarken remarked on Barrett's eloquence on pictorial composition and his admiration for the abstraction of Mondrian, while noting that Roderic's art "is decidedly not abstract; it is full of subject-matter, often mysterious and enigmatic, always strong, striking and disturbing." Although in most cases the context was "of anxiety and suffering, of human vulnerability and isolation and the ever-present threat of death," the writer realised, that any narrow interpretation was to be avoided. "To attempt to do so would destroy the mystery, the magic that stimulates artistic creation."

After Barrett's death, Puttfarken recalled an incident that illustrated "that there was never such a thing as mere formalism" in his paintings. Visiting the artist, "we looked again at a picture he had been working on for several weeks. I noticed that the figure of a little girl had been moved several inches closer to the left hand border. His explanation for this change was simple. 'I looked at her for some time and thought that she didn't want to be there.' For him the 'formal' positioning of each figure and object in an overall whole was decisively dependent upon their emotional demands within their pictorial context."

Patrizio looked at individual paintings in an endeavour to understand an artistic philosophy "built upon sincerity, personal integrity and in absorbing the best lessons in picture-making offered by great artists." He ventured that "candles, for example, surely symbolise the fragile human spirit; chairs, the physical human presence; a winged angel, death; a unicorn equates passion. But the artist himself does not often dare to second guess the impulses which have given rise to his own combinations. It is, then surely futile for us to read the unreadable, except in the sense of transcribing what we see in our own terms, and trusting our own judgement, or as Barrett might prefer it put, our own gut feelings."

Peter Freeth, who came to know his pictures over many years as a fellow-exhibitor at the Royal Academy Summer Exhibition, concluded after his death that he was sometimes uncomfortable with Roderic's work. "He was less subtle and sinewy as a painter than as a man. The assertiveness of his pictures seemed out of character, the symbolism a little pat and heavy, and there was an occasional portentousness quite unlike the open-necked, rosy-cheeked Roderic we all loved."

Just before Roderic's retrospective transferred to The Minories, he was to suffer a disappointment when Colchester Council vetoed a suggestion that work by him be bought for its art collection. The *Evening Gazette* ran a feature in which those for and against the decision to spend taxpayers' cash "on pictures of still life objects with no direct relevance to the town" expressed their views. The Council's policy was that it "should actively collect pictures illustrating the social, industrial, military and maritime nature of Colchester and district" and "contemporary topographical works with local and social relevance" the paper explained. Whereas a Council officer maintained that "the paintings were of great importance to Colchester," Councillor Rod Green insisted that a painting of a chair, for example, fell outside the Arts and Leisure Committee's policy. Thus, it was ironical that in his lifetime "my town", as Barrett called it, in which he had been brought up, had exhibited and had helped to form its Art Society, did not acquire a work by him.

After this depressing news, Barrett's spirits were raised within a few months when Essex University offered to bestow on him an honorary doctorate. "It was an absolute total surprise to me, and I wrote back and said that I was delighted and bewildered in about equal measure." In his address at the ceremony in July, 1997, the Chancellor of the University, Lord

Nolan, concluded his survey of Barrett's career that they were there to "honour a fine painter and a pillar of the humane modern art of this century." Roderic later much regretted that both at the Barbican and at the degree ceremony he had had the chance of saying something publicly, but his shyness and hatred of public performing prevented him. "I am a coward and funked doing it. It was a marvellous opportunity to say in public how much I was grateful to Lorna, my family and friends." A picture by Roderic from the University collection was hung in the presentation building for the occasion.

Gratifying as it was for Barrett to receive the Essex University honour, it would have been out of character if it had made any difference to the man. When Joan Ellis, interviewing Roderic on tape for the project Colchester Recalled, said: "So you are now *Doctor* Roderic Barrett," he rejoined ironically "and deserving of a great deal of respect." Sending memories of Roderic to the author, Peter Freeth adding RA to his name commented "if you want letters – I see Roderic shudder!…. Arrogance, pretentiousness, hypocrisy – these were Roderic's pet hates. You could imagine him howling 'vanity of vanities; all is vanity', and then laughing at himself."

Roderic had two more solo exhibitions in his lifetime. There was one at The Minories in 1999 and the 80th Anniversary at Chappel Galleries in March 2000, eight months before his death. As is routinely the case with worthwhile and enlightening exhibitions held outside London, metropolitan critics were unavailable for comment and it was left in both instances to the regional press to provide coverage. In an extensive review of Roderic's new work at The Minories, Sonia Carvill drew attention to his canvas *Celebrating*. For her, it was "bursting with life, colourful, joyous and exuberant. It had the stamp of genius…. I was haunted by its vitality." *Song and Dance* was "an astounding painting … more theatrical than a West End show."

Roderic Barrett died in Colchester on November 17, 2000. He was the third of the four brothers to die, Alex being the first, in 1981, followed by Connor in 1987 and Hugh in 2001. They had all forged distinctive careers. By the time of his death, Roderic had good cause to feel satisfied with his achievement as painter and teacher, being represented in public collections in London and the provinces and extensively in British and foreign private collections. However, it seems unlikely that he would have been satisfied, being such a perfectionist. Also, his son Mark feels that for his

father there was an underlying feeling that, "whereas in most occupations if somebody pays you that means that what you're doing is useful, if as an artist you spend many solitary hours producing pictures that nobody buys it can be seen as self-indulgent. That was a big issue with him."

Barrett received substantial illustrated obituaries in the London broadsheet newspapers and regional press. Colchester Art Society's *newsletter* carried several tributes to its third-only president in well over 50 years. In 2002, to accompany the Society's late summer exhibition, a memorial bench was unveiled at The Minories, with a plaque on it to Roderic, and a tree was planted.

In the few years since Roderic's death, his pictures have continued to excite interest. During the year that he died, his work *Family Breakfast* was used for publicity in an English Heritage, Norfolk Museums Service and York Civic Trust touring exhibition to York, Fairfax House; London, Kenwood House; and Norwich, Assembly House. The picture was also part of the illustration for the book of the same name, *Eat, Drink & Be Merry: The British at Table 1600–2000*, edited by Ivan Day. Other events followed. The show Celebrating Man: Remembering Roderic Barrett was held at Essex University Gallery in 2002. In 2003, an extensive memorial exhibition was held at Chappel Galleries.

David Buckman 2003

(below, European Parliament, Strasbourg, from left: Frank Blackmore OBE, Roderic Barrett, Lorna Barrett, Anne McIntosh MEP, Waj Mirecki, Edna Mirecka)

THE PAINTINGS
and Drawings

studio props   photograph Doug Atfield 2003

1. Self Portrait
oil   c.1937   37 x 28cm

2. Love   oil   c.1940   69 x 75cm

3. Brown Bird
oil   c.1950   75 x 69cm

4. Don Quixote and Sancho Panza VIII   oil   1948   61 x 51cm

5. Bathers (I)   oil   1947   size unknown

6. Don Quixote and Sancho Panza VI   oil   1947   103 x 69cm

7. Don Quixote and Sancho Panza   oil   c.1940s   46 x 23cm

8. Don Quixote   oil   c.1940s   76 x 51cm

9. Chairs and Table   oil   1952   69 × 51 cm

10. Men under Chairs   oil   c.1946   size unknown

11. Child Asleep   oil   c.1954   48 × 60cm

12. Ass and Man   oil   1951–52   86 × 80cm

14. Cock and Fox   oil   c.1950   41 x 71cm

13. King Herod and the Cock
oil   1946   44 x 34cm

15. Deserted House with Two Jeering Characters (a decoration)   oil   1950   61 x 92cm

16. Three Dead Rabbits
oil   1951   66 x 54cm

17. Mother and Children   oil   1951   92 × 92cm

18. The Drummer   oil   1958   122 × 92cm

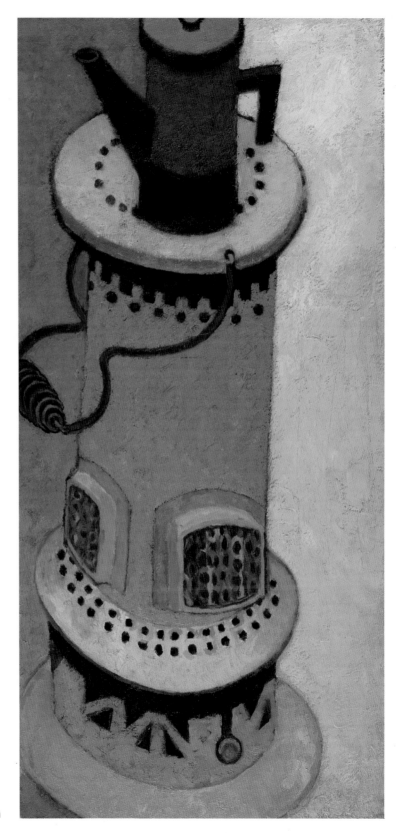

19. Oil Stove with Coffee Pot   oil   c.1950, 96   92 x 43cm

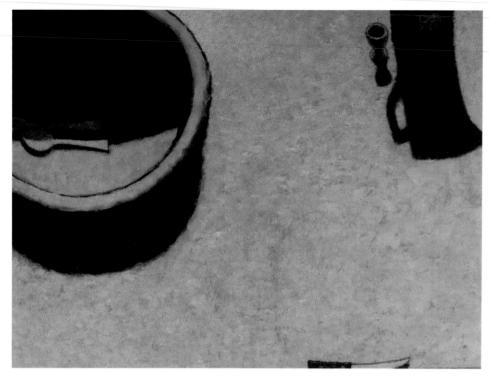

20. Bowl with Jug   oil   1951   59 x 76cm

21. Man with Wheelbarrow   oil   c.1950   45 x 45cm

22. The Gardener   oil   1953   61 x 46cm

23. Bike Ride   oil   1952–54   92 x 41cm

24. Child With Bone   oil   1953   76 x 31cm

25. Men at Table I   oil   date and size unknown

26. Men at Table II or Men Eating Under Table
oil   1953   89 x 71cm

7. Child under Chair   oil   1954   51 × 61cm

28. Family Breakfast   oil   1951   76 × 61cm

29. Familiars (Five Candles) oil 1954–56, 1959–61 153 x 122cm known version

29a. Familiars (Six Candles) oil 1954–56, 1959–61 153 x 122cm

29b. Familiars (Seven Candles) oil 1954–56, 59–61 153 x 122cm

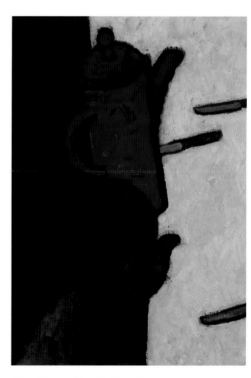

0. Journeys oil   1954–56   92 x 122cm

31. Man with Coffee Pot
oil   1954–65   51 x 36cm

32. Harvest   oil   c.1954   92 × 112cm

33. Parade (a folly
oil   1955–56
76 × 122cm

34. Three Part Dance   oil   1956–66   122 x 92cm   (known version)

34a. Three Part Dance
oil   1956–66   122 x 92cm

35. Sleeping Child   oil   1956   51 x 61cm

36. Fallen Armchair I   oil   1957   107 x 92cm

38. Fallen Armchair III   oil   1958, 69   81 x 92cm

37. Fallen Armchair II
oil   1957, 69, 82   47 x 57cm

39. Fallen Chair
oil   1957   92 x 71cm

40. The Round Table (with child) I   oil   c.1957   112 x 92cm

41. Round Table (with child)   oil   c.1957   size unknown

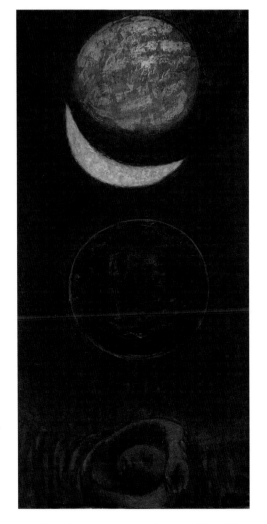

42. The Sleeper   oil   1961   137 x 69cm

43. Child at Round Table   oil   1959   130 x 83cm

44. Moon and Cot   oil   c.1959   92 x 92cm

45. Jug and Saucepan   oil   1959   31 x 76cm

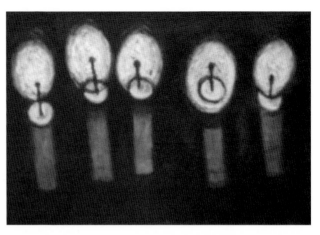

46. Candles   oil   1958–60   36 x 53cm

47. Journey   oil   1956, 98   76 x 122cm

48. Attenders I   oil   1959–61   122 x 153cm

49. Attenders II   oil   1959–66   122 x 153cm

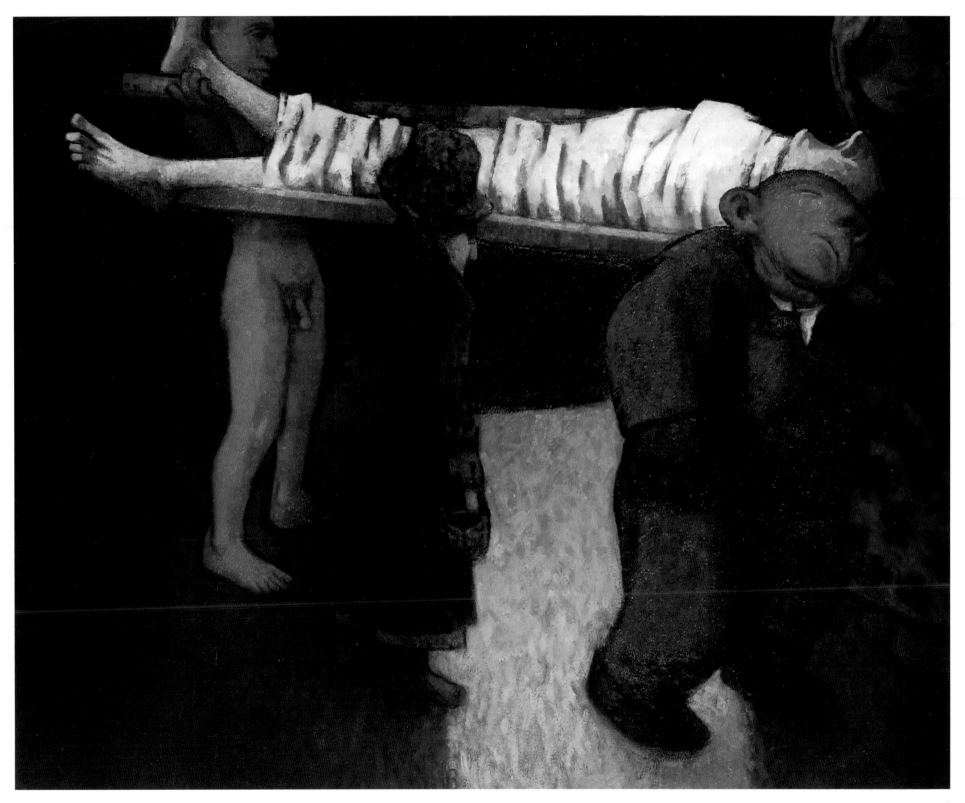

50. Burial Party   oil   1961–67, 78, 92–93   122 x 153cm

51. Morning Table   oil   1960   92 × 41cm

52. Dance in Three Parts   oil   1960   122 × 92cm

53. Round Table with Three Chairs   oil   1961–64   122 x 76cm

54. Boy at Piano   oil   c.1961   76 x 76cm

55. Chairs with Tea Cosy
oil 1960 46 x 112cm

56. Waiting Chairs
oil 1961 76 x 122cm

57. Chair and Table   oil   c.1971   76 x 92cm

58. Chair with Table   oil   1962–70   92 x 107cm

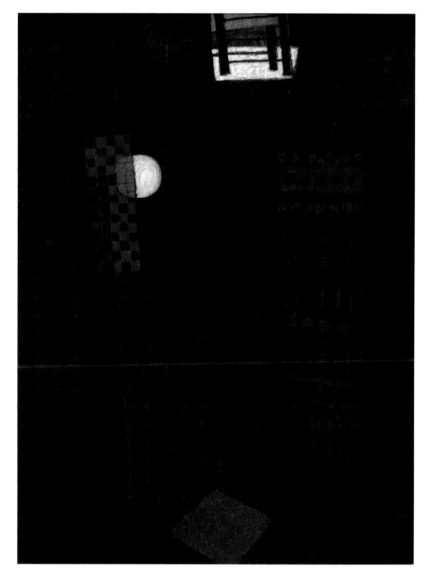

59. Singing Upstairs   oil   1959–62   122 x 92cm

60. Two Saucepans   oil   c.1960s   31 x 48cm

61. Sleeping Chair   oil   1960–61   51 x 76cm

62. Fallen Chair with Rush Seat
oil   1962   61 x 76cm

63. Tragic Puppet I
oil   1961–62   41 × 48cm

64. Broken Puppet
oil   1961–72, 93   92 × 122cm

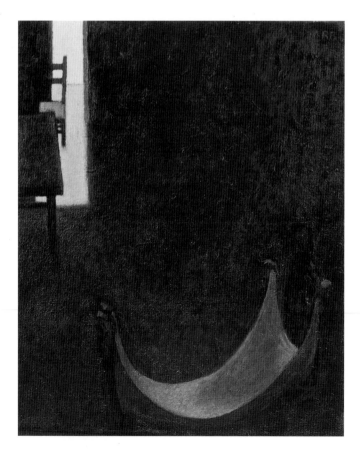

65. Doorway   oil   c.1960s   61 x 51cm

66. Eleven to Twelve   oil   c.1965   122 x 107cm

7. Watching and Reaching   oil   1962–69, 71–77   122 x 92cm

68. Kneeling, Watching, Reaching   oil   1962–65   122 x 92cm

69. Jug with Moon   oil   1963, 70   122 x 61 cm

69a. Jug and Plate   oil   1963, 70   122 x 61 cm

70. Conversation   oil   1964–67   122 x 92cm

71. Jug with Round Table   oil   1963–64   71 x 92cm

72. Candle Hat   oil   1965–69   104 x 66cm

73. Three Bowls   oil   c.1962–3   122 × 92cm

74. Harvest Field (with Sun)   oil   1962   92 × 92cm

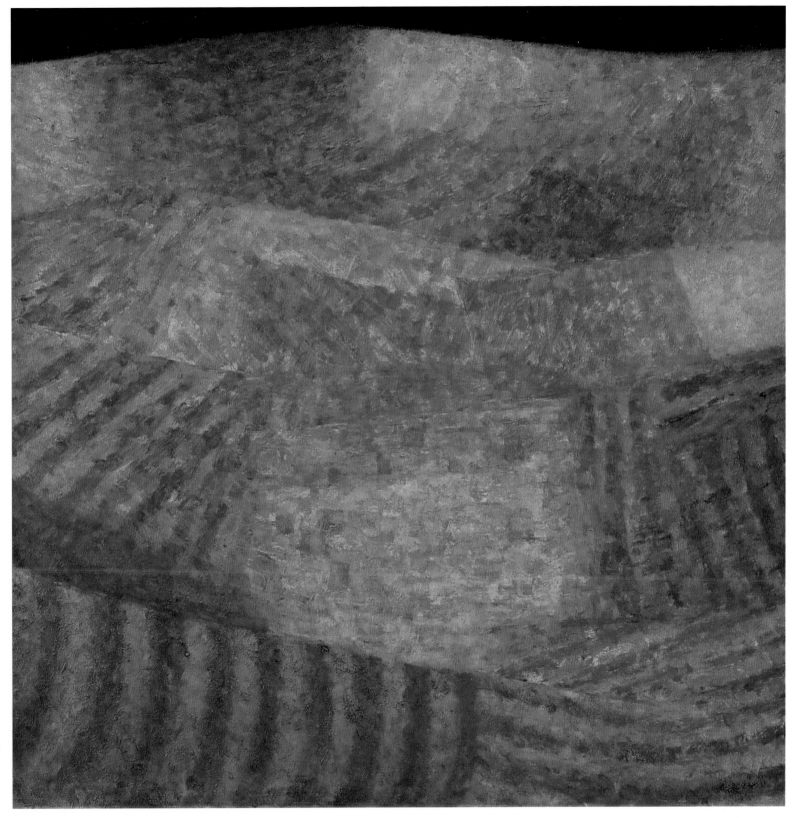

75. Golden Valley
oil
1960–62, 67
92 x 92cm

76. Old Woman with Bowls   oil   1965–69   122 x 122cm

77. Old Woman with Bowls
oil   c.1960s   46 x 46cm

78. Old Woman and Plates   oil   1966–69   122 x 122cm

79. Peeling Potatoes   oil   1964–65, 96   117 x 71cm

80. Man on Chair I
oil   1964–69   70 x 30cm

81. Man on Chair II   oil   1968–69   107 x 92cm

82. Counter Keepers   oil   1964–68   122 x 107cms

83. Oil Stove with Skull 2
oil   1966–70   71 x 31cm

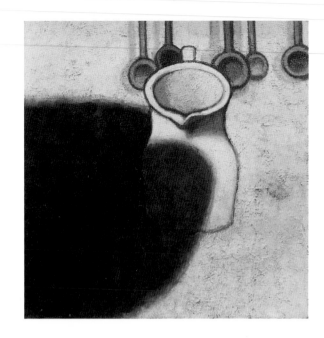

84. Jug with Darkness   oil   1969   46 x 46cm

85. Round Table with Plates   oil   1962   92 x 92cm

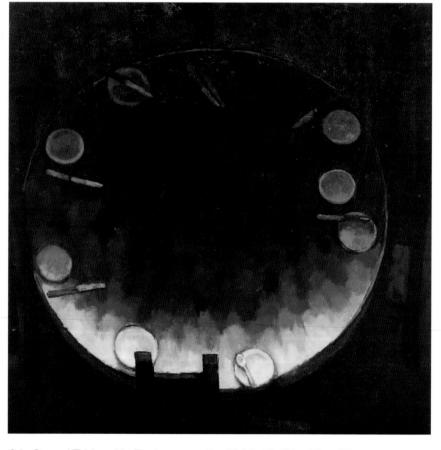

86. Round Table with Darkness   oil   1964–68, 87   92 x 92cm

87. Birthday Cake II   oil   1966–68   137 x 69cm

88. Saucepans and Tables   oil   1967–71   122 x 92cm

89. Silences III   oil   1967–71   122 × 137cm

90. Silences II   oil   1967–70   31 × 36cm

1. Stairs and Chair   oil   1969   61 x 51cm

92. Visitor   oil   1968–72, 91   122 x 122cm

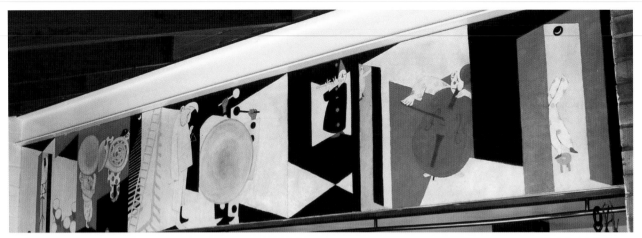

93. Clowns   oil   1966   71 x 400cm

94. The Red Blanket
oil   1968–70   122 x 153cm

5. Burnt Stubble   oil   1969   43 × 31cm

6. Field at Copford   oil   c.1969   43 × 36cm

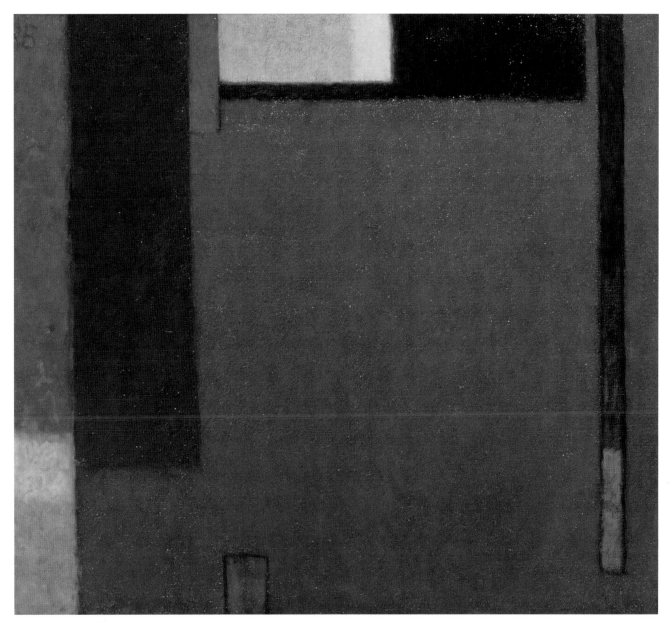

97 Moonlight Upstairs   oil   1969–75, 85   81 × 92cm

98. Footballers   oil   c.1960   89 × 59cm

99. Untitled commission
oil   c.1960s   86 × 27cm

100. Fable oil 1968–73 122 × 51 cm

101. Dream oil 1972 92 × 51 cm

102. Table and Chairs   pencil   c.1970s   36 x 34cm

103. Jugs   pencil   1973   23 x 27cm

104. Rider   oil   1970–76, 95–96   122 x 153cm

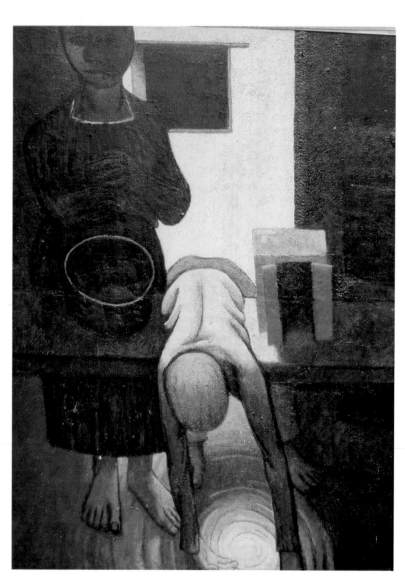

105. Reaching, Waiting   oil   1972   121 x 90cm

106. Separate Relations   oil   1970–72, 75   122 x 122cm

107. Silences I   oil   1970   122 x 122cm

108. Young Man and Old   oil   1970   122 x 92cm

109. Bowl oil 1969–71 122 x 71cm

110. Bread
oil 1970–72
122 x 51cm

111. Time Keeper
oil
1973–76, 83
92 × 92cm

112. A Cock for Aesculapius
oil   1973–78   92 x 92cm

113. Interior   oil   1967–68   92 x 92cm

114. Parade of Talents   oil   1971–73   137 x 153cm

115. Parade of Talents   oil   1971–73–77   137 × 153cm

116. Companions   oil   1972, 88   153 × 81cm

117. Don Quixote and Sancho Panza
oil   c.1970   62 x 46cm

118. Everyday Dance   oil   1973–77   137 x 153cm

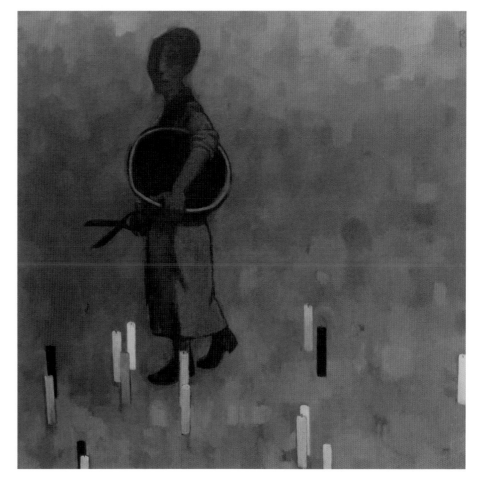

19. Bit Part Players   oil   1972, 96   122 x 122cm

120. Scissors Woman   oil   1971–75, 86   122 x 122cm

121. Barrett's Circus I   oil   1973   51 x 76cm

122. Man with Wheelbarrow   oil   1972   92 x 122cm

123. Visitor   oil   c.1960s   30 x 25cm   124. Household   oil   1971–73   122 x 153cm

127. Bread and Knife   pencil   1973   23 x 39cm

125. Jug and Papers
pencil   1974   36 x 20cm

126. Paper and Candle   pencil   1973   23 x 41cm

128. Breadknife and Teaspoons
pencil   c.1970s   34 x 20cm

29. City Road   oil   1973–77   132 x 221cm

130. A Little Scene   oil   1976–78   31 x 33cm

131. Outside Interior   oil   c.1970s   61 x 76cm

32. View of a Death   oil   1975–79, 88   137 x 213cm

133. Covering   oil   1974–77, 82   142 x 66cm

134. Chair with Child   oil   1975–85, 99   122 x 61cm

135. Umbrella oil c.1977 153 × 92cm

136. Umbrella Man oil 1974–77, 81 137 × 69cm

138. Dark Umbrella
oil   c.1960s   36 x 25cm

139. Old Friends Going 1
oil   c.1970s   size unknown

137. Fool for a Moon   oil   1978–80   122 x 76cm

140. People and Things   oil   1979–83   76 x 76cm

141. Singing Together Downhill   oil   1977–80, 88, 99   107 x 92cm

142. George and Charlie (Duo for)   oil   1976–78   122 x 92cm

143. Jug and Tea Cosy   pencil   c.1973   23 x 33cm

144. Jug and Bread   pencil   1974   25 x 35cm

145. Chair with Candle   oil   1978–80   92 x 107cm

46. Candles for Dead Friends   oil   1977–80   102 × 183cm

147. A Chair in its Place   oil   1977–80   122 x 122cm

148. Cock for Aesculapius (Death of Socrates)
oil   1979–82, 88   122 x 122cm

149. Inseparables   oil   1979–81   122 x 153cm

150. The Moon's Shadow   oil   c.1980   53 × 36cm

151. Fool and Moon   oil   c.1980   76 × 51cm

152. Travelling Show
oil   1980–83, 91
122 x 122cm

153. Players oil 1981–84, 90 137 x 153cm

154. Three Players
oil 1982–90 99 x 48cm

155. Enter Two Characters   oil   1980–85   122 x 61cm

156. Stage   oil   1981, 91   153 x 137cm

157. Curtain Call   oil   1981–84   122 x 153cm

158. Kitchen   oil   1983–85   56 × 92cm

159. Man with Wheelbarrow
oil   1983–86   51 × 61cm

160. *Early to Rise*
(Book Cover)
oil   1982   31 × 28cm

161. Dustbin Lid with Pail   oil   1984–86   61 × 81cm

162. Bath, Lid and Pail   oil   1984–86   66 × 81cm

163. The Arts, Army, Church Dance   oil   1982–84   76 x 89cm

164. Conversation
oil   1987   36 x 15cm

165. Them and Us   oil   1985–91, 92   109 x 191 cm

166. Unknown title
oil   c.1980s   size unknown

167. Passage
oil   1985–90   71 x 127cm

68. Chair with Hat
oil 1986–88 61 x 56cm

169. Hauntings oil 1987–91 92 x 122cm

170. Red Door   oil   c.1988   71 x 71cm

171. Stage Hand   oil   c.1987   38 x 51cm

133">133

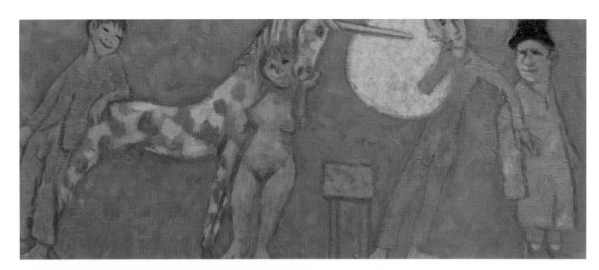

172. Apricot
oil   1986–88   31 x 71cm

173. Procession
oil   1987, 90, 93–94   102 x 122cm

174. Skull and Hat   oil   1987–89   41 × 76cm

175. Four at Table   oil   1989–94   153 × 137cm

176. Painter at Work   oil   1987–88   69 x 48cm

177. Entertainers   oil   1989, 99   92 x 92cm

178. Celebration   oil   1990–93, 99   122 x 76cm

179. A Little More Light Conversation
oil   1995–96   102 x 66cm

180. Trundling and Juggling   oil   1991–96   92 × 122cm

181. Celebrating Man   oil   1990–95   122 x 153cm

182. A Little Light Conversion
oil   c.1993   61 x 36cm

83. Death, Maid and Joker   oil   1993–95   91 x 122cm

184. Remembered Bedtime   oil   1993, 95–99   102 x 102cm

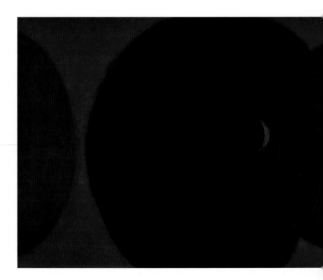

185. Old Time   oil   1993–96   46 x 56cm

186. A Drummer and His Muse   oil   1995–97   122 x 81cm

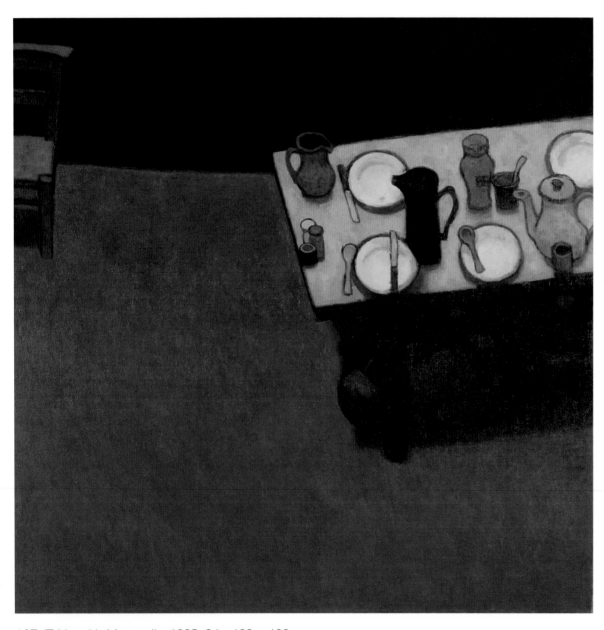

187. Table with Man   oil   1995–96   122 x 122cm

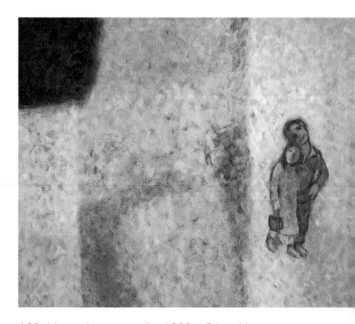

188. Young Lovers   oil   1999   51 x 61cm

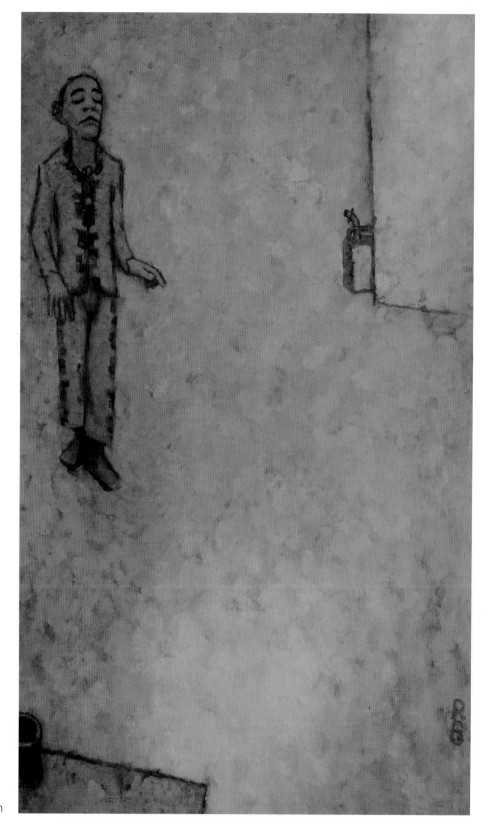

189. Fool Surprised by Light   oil   1993, 95–00   122 x 76cm

190. Bike Riding Man   oil   1995–98   92 x 71cm

191. Messengers   oil   1996–99   137 x 153cm

192. Song and Dance   oil   1994–97   137 x 153cm

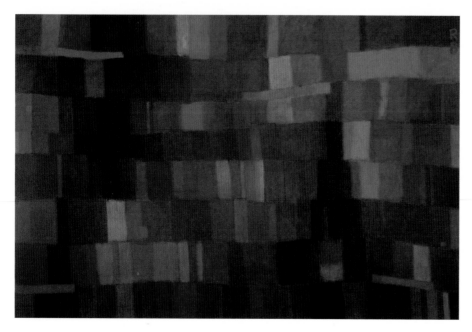

193. A Long Day's Walk   oil   1996–99   102 x 153cm

194. Good Samaritan   oil   1997–00   137 x 183cm

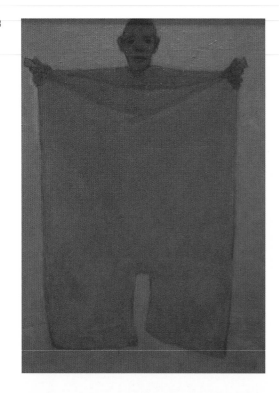

195. Man Holding Sheet   oil   c.1999   51 × 36cm

196. End Place   oil   1996–98   69 × 137cm

197. A Clown Introducing Three Fundamentalists   oil   1997–99   137 x 153cm

198. Family Tree   oil   1999   183 x 92cm

199. Bath and Pails
oil   c.1999
92 × 92cm

200. Work in progress   oil   1999   153 x 153cm

201. Chair with Pail
oil 1997–99 102 x 92cm

AHEAD OF THE LIGHT
THE WOOD ENGRAVINGS OF RODERIC BARRETT

"There is nothing like a printed black . . . it has a different kind of body." In 1924 Paul Nash illustrated the first chapter of *Genesis*; portraying in 12 engravings the seven days of the creation. The black block of the first, *The Void* has only the faintest crosshatchings in the top corners to indicate the coming of the light. So it was with Roderic Barrett's most profound engravings: letting light into the void, with their creator a little ahead of that light. Barrett never concealed his admiration for, or the influence of, Meninsky and Roberts who taught him life-drawing at the Central. But John Farleigh, his instructor in wood engraving, self-conscious and a consummate craftsman, was his only master. The relationship, though formal, was based on an unspoken similarity of outlook, metaphorical imagery and a certain shared melancholia.

It is evident that Barrett had begun printmaking in lino while still at school, filling his surface with large chunky figures or other oversize compositional elements. Farleigh's contemporary work: *The Way of All Flesh* (1934), *The Man who Died* (1935), *John the Baptist* (1936) *et al* are all referenced in the teenager's early work: *Two Angels and Man*, *Man with Aura*, *Man and Plant* and in the ten illustrations for William Cobbett's *Rural Rides*. *Two Men, One Sleeping* is the young pacifist's response to the coming war in terms of the last; the elongated body of one figure and the 'outframed' torso of the other may be derived from Farleigh, but were later to be exploited as personal metaphors. The vignetted Shakespearean headpieces engraved by the 18-year-old show a grasp of learned and communicated craftsmanship and variety far ahead of their years; while the 'fineness' of *Falstaff* and the hunched monumentality of other *dramatis personae* of *Henry IV* still have something of Farleigh in them, they already show a maturity way in advance of the Cobbett. Four engravings in particular of 1938–9: *Big Sad Dog*, *Boy Asleep*, *All that Should Be* and *Boy* all show the influence of Farleigh's monumental engravings *Melancholia* (1935) and *Lilith* (1937), but the subject is entirely Barrett's own; himself – and the uncontrolled emotions, wistfulness and yearning of youth. Sixty years later when writing a short essay to illustrate *Boy* for *More who do . . . and One who did* (Bishops Books 1999) he claimed that no sooner had he taken the first proof of this block than 'I could see that the flowers, the part I had been most certain of, were wrong. Alas,

I could do nothing to change these mistakes . . . so painting in oils became the means that best suited me [in which] I could make changes, weeks . . . or months after thinking a work complete.' While in the final analysis this judgement may be right, and painting did become the means to the right ends, there is also something *post facto* about it. It shows Barrett's capacity to mislead, to explain the past in terms of the present. In fact, *Boy* with the lost engraving *Summer* (could this be one of the extant prints re-titled?) became the young artist's first exhibited prints at the original Society of Wood Engravers' (SWE) last annual exhibition in 1939–40. The two works (of only 103 selected) shared wall space with Farleigh, Blair Hughes-Stanton, Gertrude Hermes, John Buckland Wright, Eric Ravilious, Ian Macnab, Agnes Miller Parker and Clifford Webb – the finest at their best.

In 1940 in the allegorical engraving *The Blue Bird* the farewell to youth and love comes with the realisation that letting-go, the melancholy of unrequited love, is part of the human condition. As an engraving it begins, for this 20-year-old, the pivot from which the later mature work would spring. Its immediate precursor, his unique etching *Love*, is based on George de La Tour's *Madonna and Child*, a painting Barrett much admired, for its stillness and darkness-illuminating light; as he would later say that 'though the figures have an earthiness about them which speaks to our own sense of weight, all is mysterious'. *Love* when considered in these terms fails; it probably cost Barrett too much in emotion to suppress it, but in engraving *The Blue Bird* he knew he had got it right: so much so that when he painted the large *Brown Bird* a decade later it is identical in composition and detail, only reversed from the print – i.e., as on the block – and the girl's thumb slightly remodelled.

Seven years of war and directed labour did not blunt the artist, although it offered little opportunity for printmaking; the enigmatic linocut *King Herod and the Cock* is a strikingly taut and controlled work, the monumental brutality of the soldiers in contrast to the fluid shifting shapes of *Figures*. Farleigh rescued Barrett, inviting him back to the Central School, to teach, in 1947; within a decade the instructor of drawing and design would achieve unparalleled and international recognition as an engraver, develop archetypes and a repertory of players and objects – and having done so transfer them to paint and abandon print altogether. Amongst the earliest and most universal; the man and child appear in *Traveller*. The man is grounded in light, supporting the boy who, still a child, sees but the dark until led into the light. All engraving from now until its abandonment and much of the later painting are depictions of that journey from darkness into light before the darkness comes again; or fleeting moments and encounters on the journey's way. The rare self-referential *Painter* seems to be a work of encouragement, head bowed in reverence before the naked and stricken man who is exposed to flickering tongues of light (see page 18 Pas Seul); the painting suspended between distinct planes – imagery so simple yet conveying a multiplicity of messages. The tube of paint floatingly balanced on the table will be echoed and re-echoed in paint until the final stagecall.

Barrett's capacity as an artist *and* craftsman to animate the block and to create profound images from types, and forms from ideas be they the *Family Bike Ride*, the *Family House* or the strange *Don Quixote and the Cock* (also mirrored in painting) is matched by the versatility and diversity of those images. One of the startling truths about Barrett's wood engraving is not that he couldn't change it but that he got it right so easily and so young. Elected the youngest full member of the reformed SWE in 1951 he exhibited *Ass and Man* and *Journey* in their first show since the war in that year. While one shows a full assimilation of the international avant garde the other is the very essence of the man: on a journey, ahead of the light. Chairs in various guises are a re-occurring motif: *Sleeping Chair*, *Chairs and Men*, *Fallen Chair* and *Family of Chairs*, and became a central part of the sparse idiom of Barrett the painter. One senses that just as the paintings were constantly re-arranged, altered, corrected and *reformed* in the search for perfect expression of the idea, 'getting it right', the different blocks were a precursor to this process of reformation. But altering the idea of the engraving meant engraving anew, a block cannot be reformed in the way paint can be applied and wiped out at will. Nevertheless the enigmatic character of the engravings only continued in the paintings. What do these fallen, grouped and sleeping chairs mean? (see Chapter 6 para. 6) *Sleeping Chair* is such a disparate displacement in space that it is almost entirely abstract. It has been suggested that in the painter's private mythology they serve as the physical human presence, though in the fallen and sleeping variants they may simply point up spiritual absence – in both the central subject has gone. Even in *Chairs and Men* the men seem to be vanishing, their presence literally framed in the pattern beyond and behind the chair. Barrett uses a formal idiom to engrave a print or paint a picture,

but declines to use formal language to elucidate; as viewers we must accept them as images, not ask what they mean. The question thus becomes, has he succeeded as an engraver in creating a print that invites us to look at at?

The colour linocut *Deserted House with Two Jeering Figures* exhibited with the SWE in 1955 (the figures were not jeering then!) and internationally in 1956 seems to be one of the points of transfer from print to paint. The recently found *Visitor*, which disturbs not in its abstraction but with its sense of a dreadful annunciation, was to be repeated in paintings. *Couple, Child and Candles* is the closest engraving to the later canvases with its direct painterly approach and compositional types. It achieves a warm emotional truth.

By 1961 the painter's impulse was visceral, Barrett was already throwing his critics off the scent, telling them he made engravings from paintings when the truth was the opposite. In 1953 John Buckland Wright had called him the most outstanding engraver of the younger generation 'by far . . . showing rare vision and invention'. The abandonment of wood engraving removed an engraver who fully engaged with the language of modernism while imposing on it his own unique vocabulary, bringing the post-war avant-garde to the medium, while the medium itself was slipping from fashion. As a painter Barrett continued with his same insistent concerns, portraying an inner world conceived as symbolic, a metaphysical mélange of alienation and not a little sorrow. As an engraver there is very little alienation, with perfected form there is very little insistence on creating tableaux, the prints are open images. Having remained unseen for nearly 40 years it is good that they are back in the light and still ahead of it.

Hal Bishop

202. Cecil Barrett   wood engraving   c.1930   5.5 × 5cm

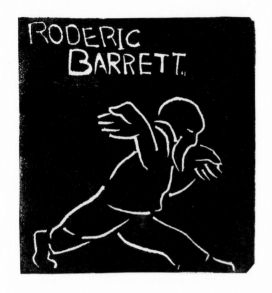

203. Striding
linocut 1934–35 7 x 6.5cm

204. Strongman
linocut 1934–35 11.5 x 8.5cm

205. Two Men Gesticulating
linocut 1935 size unknown

206. St Christopher Magazine 1935
line drawing   1935 (printed)   30 x 22cm

207. St Christopher Magazine July 1935
line drawing and repeat design   1935 (printed)   30 x 22cm

208. Man with Book   lino/woodcut   c.1935   19 x 14cm

209. Man in Trees
lino/woodcut   c.1935   8 x 9cm

210. Man in Tempest
woodcut   c.1936   13 x 10cm

211. Tree with Fence
woodcut   c.1935–36   18 x 13cm

212. Tree and Diagonal River
woodcut   c.1936   15 x 11cm

213. Group with Sun
woodcut   c.1936   10 x 8cm

214. Large and Small Figure   lino/woodcut   c.1936   reduced from 29 x 23cm

215. A Man in the Woods
lino/woodcut   c.1936
9 x 8cm

216. Landscape
lino/woodcut   c.1936
9 x 5cm

217. Patriarch
lino/woodcut   c.1936
13 x 8cm

218. Man Looking Up Tree   wood engraving   1936   10 x 7.5cm

219. Two Angels and Man
wood engraving 1936 12 x 11cm

220. Man in Pond
woodcut/engraving 1936 15.5 x 10cm

221. Tramp wood engraving 1936 6.5 x 5cm

222. Two Farmworkers   wood engraving   1936–37   16 x 12.5cm

223. Man and Plant   wood engraving   1936–37   14 x 10cm

224. Man with Aura   wood engraving   1936–37   17.5 x 12.5cm

225. Man in Swirl   wood engraving   1936–37   15 x 10cm

226. Man Hailing Weather
wood engraving   1936–37   12 x 10cm

227. Five Figures lino/woodcut 1936–37 reduced from 28 x 20cm

228. Tombstones   wood engraving   c.1937   15.5 x 10cm

229. Bridge over Stream
wood engraving   c.1937   14 x 10cm

Cobbett's Rural Rides nos 230 to 238

230. Farmstead   wood engraving   1937   14 x 11cm

231. Two Figures on Hill above Farmstead
wood engraving   1937   14 x 11cm

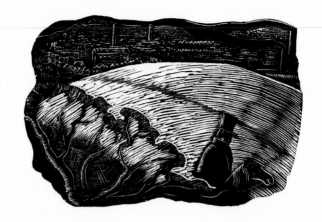

232. Farmer on Horse with Two Trees
wood engraving   1937   5 x 8.5cm

233. Farmer on Horse
wood engraving   1937   5 x 7.5cm

234. Farmer Leading Horse
wood engraving   1937   7.5 x 11cm

235. Two Men and Cart Horse
wood engraving   1937   7.5 x 11cm

236. Men Carrying Sacks   wood engraving   1937   6.5 × 11cm

237. Men Going Through Door   wood engraving   1937   7.5 × 11cm

238. Village   wood engraving   1937   8.5 × 11cm

239. Engraving for War Poem   wood engraving   1937   10 x 14cm

240. Drink by Candlelight   wood engraving   c.1937   12.5 x 18cm

241. Boy with Girl
wood engraving   c.1937   10 x 14cm

242. Woman
wood engraving   c.1937   14 x 10cm

243. Woodland Forms   wood engraving   c.1937   6 x 5cm

244. Eight Figures   linocut   c.1937   reduced from 28 x 21cm

245. Two Tragic Figures – Lear
wood engraving   1937   14 x 7.5cm

246. After Bellini
wood engraving   1937   reduced from 28 x 21cm

247. Head with Five Figures   linocut   c.1937   reduced from 29 x 23cm

248 Falstaff, Henry IV   wood engraving   1938   18 x 12cm

249. Four figures in the style of Henry IV   wood engraving   1938   18 x 11cm

250. Henry IV (seven figures)   wood engraving   1938   18 x 12cm

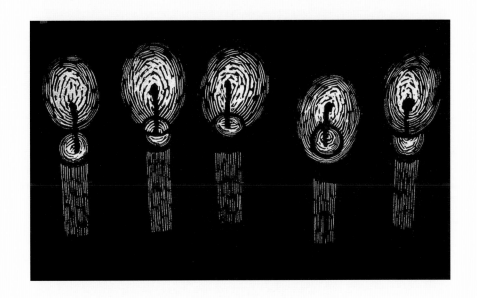

251. Henry IV   wood engraving   1938   8 x 11.5cm

252.   Five Candles   wood engraving   c.1950s   7 x 11.5cm

253. Big Sad Dog   wood engraving   1938   18 x 11.5cm

254. Boy Asleep   wood engraving   1938   reduced from 23 x 15cm

255. All That Should Be   wood engraving   1938   reduced from 27 x 21cm

256. Boy   wood engraving   1939   15 x 23cm

258. Behold the Mother and Child
linocut   1938–40   12 x 9cm

259. Father, mother, child
wood engraving   1939–40   size unknown

257. Don Quixote and Sancho Panza   wood engraving   1939–40   20 x 13cm

261, 262. Colour versions
30.5 x 23.5cm

260. King Herod and the Cock   linocut   1946   30.5 x 23.5cm

263. Love   etching   1939   15 x 17cm

264. The Blue Bird   wood engraving   1940   18.5 x 17cm

265. Traveller   wood engraving   1947   10 x 13.5cm

266. Painter   wood engraving   1948   18 x 11.5cm

267. Don Quixote and Cock
wood engraving   1950   19.5 x 6.5cm

268. Figure   linocut   1949   reduced from 27 x 26.5cm

269. Ass and Man (yellow version)
wood engraving   1951   18.5 x 17cm

270. Ass and Man   wood engraving   1951   18.5 x 17cm

271. Journey   wood engraving   1951   19.5 x 25cm

CALENDAR 1951-2

AGRICULTURAL CONTRACTORS LIMITED

SUDBURY, SUFFOLK

This opportunity is gladly taken of acknowledging the
wide and generous response that is accorded the A.C.L.
calendars by friends near and far. Such a volume of appreciation, criticism and suggestion is the greatest encouragement possible. Gratitude must also be expressed to Roderic
Barrett, who undertook the six wood engravings of speci-
mens he gathered from the neighbourhood of the quarries,
and to the printers, Benham and Co. Ltd., who, with other
friends, collaborated in the present issue.

ACL Calendar engravings nos. 272 to 277

272. Whitebeam   wood engraving   c.1951   8 x 13cm

273. Yew   wood engraving   c.1951   19 x 8cm
reproduced from printed calendar

274. Dog Rose   wood engraving   c.1951   8 x 13cm

275. Spindle   wood engraving   c.1951   18 x 8cm

276. Beech   wood engraving   c.1951   8 x 13cm

277. Dogwood
wood engraving   c.1951   18 x 8cm

278. Chairs and Men   wood engraving   1952   reduced from 26 x 21cm

280. Family House
wood engraving 1952 7.5 x 7cm

279. Family Bike Ride
wood engraving 1952 18 x 8cm

281. Family of Chairs
wood engraving 1950–55 6 x 9.5cm

282. Sleeping Chair   wood engraving   1950–55   13.5 x 22.5cm

283. Cock and Fox   wood engraving   c.1950s   11.5 x 17.5cm

284. King and Candle   wood engraving   c.1950s   7 x 7.5cm

283. Two Heads   lino/woodcut   c.1950s   9.5 x 12.5cm

286. Deserted House with Two Jeering Characters   linocut   1955   reduced from 30 x 40cm

287. Bike Ride   linocut   c.1956   reduced from 22 x 13.5cm

288. Fallen Chair   wood engraving   1956   20 x 26cm

289. Birthday Cake   wood engraving   c.1950s   15.5 x 13cm

290. Visitor
wood engraving   c.1950s   13.5 x 7cm

INVENTORY OF OIL PAINTINGS

Apricot   1986-88   31 x 71cm   CPl.172
Phoenix Gallery 1988; Barbican/firstsite 1996-97

Arts Army Church Dance   1982-84   76 x 89cm   Pl.163
C.A.S. 1986; Epping Forest District Museum 1989; (Phoenix Gallery c.1988)
Collection: Epping Forest District Museum 1989

Ass and Man   1951-52   86 x 80cm   CPl.12
C.A.S. 1954; Beaux Arts Gallery 1954; The Lamont Gallery USA 1957; The Minories 1973; Barbican/firstsite 1996-97; (London Group)

Attenders I   1959-61   122 x 153cm   Pl.48
C.A.S. 1959; Wildenstein & Co. Ltd. 1961; Gainsborough's House 1962; King Street Gallery 1963; Alwin Gallery 1966; (Hintlesham Hall)

Attenders II   1959-66   122 x 153cm   Pl.49
C.A.S. 1966; Alwin Gallery 1967; The Minories 1973 & 84 (Cambridge 1966; University of Essex 1966)

Autumn Valley see Golden Valley

Barrett's Circus I   1973   51 x 76cm   Pl.121
The Minories 1984

Barrett's Circus 2   1975-76   92 x 122cm
Thackeray Gallery 1976

Bath and Pails   c.1999   92 x 92cm   CPl.199
Chappel Galleries 2000; University Gallery, Essex 2002

Bathers I   1947   Pl.5
The Hilton Gallery 1948

Bathers II
The Hilton Gallery 1948

Bath, Lid and Pail   1984-86   66 x 81cm   CPl.162
also known as Bath, Bucket and Lid
R.A. 1985; Christchurch Mansion 1987; C.A.S. 1987; The Epping Forest District Museum 1989; Meeanee Barracks 1992; Chappel Galleries 1993

Bike Ride also exhibited as   1952-54   92 x 41cm   Pl.23
Bicycle Ride also known as Girl and Father on Bicycle
C.A.S. 1953; Beaux Arts Gallery 1954; The Lamont Gallery USA 1957, (Shore Studio Galleries USA 1958)

Bike Riding Man   1995-98   92 x 71cm   CPl.190
Chappel Galleries 2000,03

Birthday Cake   c.1956
Beaux Arts Gallery 1956

Birthday Cake – Party   1962   122 x 61cm
King Street Gallery 1963

Birthday Cake II   1966-68   137 x 69cm   CPl.87
Alwin Gallery 1967; C.A.S. 1968; Oxford Gallery 1971; The Minories/Castle Museum Norwich 1973/74; I & J Weiss 1976; Thackeray Gallery 1976; University of Keele 1976; (Ash Barn Gallery 1970; Southampton c.1975; Warwick)

Bit Part Players   1972.rwd.96   122 x 122cm   Pl.119
Barbican/firstsite 1996-97

Bit Players   1972-73   46 x 46cm
The Minories 1973; (Ash Barn c.1970)

Blind Men   1950-51   46 x 46cm
Beaux Arts Gallery 1954; The Lamont Gallery USA 1957; The Minories 1973

Bowl   1969-71   122 x 71cm   Pl.109
R.A. 1971; Castle Museum Norwich 1974; Oxford Gallery 1975; Thackeray Gallery 1978,80

Bowls see Three Bowls

Bowl with Apple(s)
C.A.S. 1961; Gainsborough's House 1962; (Cambridge)

Bowl with Jug   1951   59 x 76cm   CPl.20
C.A.S. 1962; (Cambridge)

Boy At Piano   c.1961   76 x 76cm   Pl.54
(depicting son, Mark Barrett)
King Street Gallery 1963; Alwin Gallery 1966; (R.B.A.; Colchester)

Boy in the Sun   1943
The Hilton Gallery 1948

Bread   1970-72   122 x 51cm   CPl.110
The Minories/Castle Museum Norwich 1973/74

Broken Puppet   1961-72,rwd 93   92 x 122cm   CPl.64
also exhibited as Tragic Puppet
The Minories/Castle Museum Norwich 1973/74; Thackeray Gallery 1976; Chelmsford & Essex Museum 1979; Christchurch Mansion 1987; C.A.S. 1989; Meeanee Barracks 1992; Chappel Galleries 1993; Barbican/firstsite 1996-97; (Oxford)

Broken Puppet see Tragic Puppet I

Brown Bird   c.1950   75 x 69cm   CPl.3
Chappel Galleries 2003

Burial Party   1961-67.rwd.78   122 x 153cm   CPl.50
also exhibited: Burial   rwd.92-93
University of Essex 1966; The Hilton Gallery 1966; The Minories/Castle Museum Norwich 1973/74; Thackeray Gallery 1978; Chelmsford & Essex Museum 1979; RA 1993; Strasbourg 1995; Barbican/firstsite 1996-97; Chappel Galleries 2003; (East Anglian Art; Imperial Institute; Ipswich 1971)

Burnt Stubble   1969   43 x 31cm   Pl.95
Alwin Gallery 1970

Candle End   1962   27 x 34cm
Minories 1973; (Cambridge; University of Essex)

Candle Hat   1965-69   104 x 66cm   CPl.72
Alwin Gallery 1970; The Minories/Castle Museum Norwich 1973/74; Thackeray Gallery 1976; University of Keele 1976; Chelmsford & Essex Museum 1979; R.A. 1983; The Minories/Playhouse Gallery 1984; Ash Barn Gallery c.1970; Oxford Gallery; Phoenix Gallery c.1988; Southampton c.1975)

Candles   1958-60   36 x 53cm   CPl.46
King Street Gallery 1963; Minories/Castle Museum Norwich 1973/74; Chelmsford & Essex Museum 1979; Barbican/firstsite 1996-97;(Alwin Gallery; Ash Barn Gallery c.1970; Long Melford 1969; University of Cambridge)

Candles for Dead Friends   1977-80   102 x 183cm   CPl.146
previously known as Candles for Five Friends
also exhibited as Candles for Friends
Thackeray Gallery 1980; RA 1981 (ill); The Minories/Playhouse Gallery 1984; Chappel Galleries 1993,03; Strasbourg 1995; Barbican/firstsite 1996-97; (Oxford; Phoenix Gallery c.1988)

Celebrating Man   1990-95   122 x 153cm   CPl.181
R.A. 1995; Barbican/firstsite 1996-97; Chappel Galleries 2000; University Gallery Essex 2002

Celebration   1990-93.rwd.99   122 x 76cm   CPl.178
R.A. 1991; Meeanee Barracks 1992; C.A.S. 1992; Chappel Galleries 1993/2000; Strasbourg 1995; Barbican/firstsite 1996-97; firstsite 1999

Chair and Man (a folly) see Man and Chair

Chair and Table   c.1971   76 x 92cm   CPl.57
exhibited as Table and Chair
Oxford Gallery 1971; (Cambridge, Long Melford, Brighton)

Chair, Child and Table
also exhibited: Table, Chair and Child
Beaux Arts Gallery 1954; C.A.S. 1954

Chair In Its Place (A)   1977-80   122 x 122cm   CPl.147
R.A. 1979; Thackery Gallery 1980; The Minories/Playhouse Gallery 1984; Christchurch Mansion 1987; Barbican/firstsite 1996-97; Christchurch Mansion/firstsite 1997
Collection: Ipswich Borough Museum and Galleries purchased 1987 supported by East Anglian Arts

Chairs and Men   1955
Beaux Arts Gallery 1954; Kings Street Gallery 1963; (Colchester; Hintlesham; Sudbury)

Chairs and Table   1952   69 x 51cm   CPl.9
Beaux Arts Gallery 1954; The Lamont Gallery USA 1957; C.A.S. 1971

Chairs with Tea Cosy   1960   46 x 112cm   Pl.55
also exhibited as
Table, Chairs and Tea Cosy
Chairs and Tea Cosy
Tea Cosy
Chair with Tea Cosy
Oxford Gallery 1971; The Minories/Castle Museum Norwich 1973/74; Thackeray Gallery 1978; Chappel Galleries 1993; R.A. 1994; (Alwin; Cambridge; Colchester; Halesworth; Hintlesham; Holland Park Gallery 1964)

Chair with Candle   1978-80   92 x 107cm   CPl.145
R.A. 1978; Chelmsford and Essex Museum 1979; The Minories 1979; Thackeray Gallery 1980; The Minories 1984; Christchurch Mansion 1987; Epping Forest District Museum 1988; (Oxford; Phoenix Gallery c.1988)

Chair with Child   1975-85,99   122 x 61cm   CPl.134
also exhibited: Child in Chair
Thackeray Gallery 1978,80; Chelmsford & Essex Museum 1979; C.A.S. 1982, 87; The Minories/Playhouse Gallery 1984; Chappel Galleries 1993,00

Chair with Child   1976

Chair with Hat   1986-88   61 x 56cm   CPl.168
C.A.S. 1986; R.A. 1988; Meeanee Barracks 1992; Chappel Galleries 1993; (Phoenix Gallery c.1988)

Chair with Pail   1997-99   102 x 92cm   CPl.201
Chappel Galleries 2000,03; University Gallery, Essex 2002

Chair with Table   1962-70   92 x 107cm   Pl.58
University Gallery, Essex 1966; Alwin Gallery 1967; The Minories/Norwich Castle Museum 1973/74; Barbican/firstsite 1996-97; (Colchester; Hintlesham)

Child and Chairs see Child under Chairs

Child and Table
C.A.S. 1956; Beaux Arts Gallery 1956

Child Asleep   1954   48 x 60cm   CPl.11
C.A.S. 1956; The Lamont Gallery USA 1957; King St Gallery 1963; (Beaux Arts Gallery; Colchester)

Child at Round Table   1959   130 x 83cm   Pl.43
also known as Round Table with Child
Barbican/firstsite 1996-97; (Sudbury)

Child, Chair and Table   1956
King Street Gallery 1963

Child in a Nighty
Beaux Arts Gallery 1954

Child in Chair with Toy   1953
Beaux Arts Gallery 1954; The Lamont Gallery USA 1957; (Colchester)

Child Painting
Beaux Arts Gallery 1954; The Lamont Gallery USA 1957

Items in brackets = unconfirmed information

rwd = reworked

h.c. = highly commended

R.A. = Royal Academy, London

C.A.S. = Colchester Art Society

The Minories was purchased from Dr Ruth Bensusan-Butt 1956, and opened as an Art Gallery 30 May 1958; it has been known as firstsite since 1995.

Chappel Galleries opened 16 May 1986, proprietors Edna Mirecka (Battye) and Wladyslaw Mirecki.

DRAWINGS

Abandoned Coat 1973 36 x 23cm
The Minories 1973

Apple Tree 1970 20 x 29.5cm
The Minories 1973

Bath and Sickle 1970 24 x 32cm
The Minories 1973

Bath, Hat and Books 1973 29.5 x 38cm
Castle Museum Norwich 1974

Bit Player 1971 24 x 36cm
The Minories/Castle Museum Norwich 1973/74

Bit Players 1971 26.5 x 36cm
The Minories/Castle Museum Norwich 1973/74

Bone, Hat and Plimsoles 1973 36 x 25cm
University of Keele 1976

Boots
The Minories 1984; Chappel Galleries 1991

Boots and Hat 1973 29.5 x 21.5cm
C.A.S. 1979; Christchurch Mansion 1987

Bowl 21.5 x 23cm
Oxford Gallery 1971

Bread 1970 34.5 x 20cm
The Minories/Castle Museum Norwich 1973/74

Bread and Eggcup 23 x 38cm
C.A.S. 1984; Christchurch Mansion 1987; The Playhouse Gallery 1984; C.A.S. Spons.

Bread and Jug 1972 25 x 33cm
University of Keele 1976

Bread and Knife 1973 23 x 39cm Pl.127
The Minories/Castle Museum Norwich 1973/74; University of Keele 1976

Bread, Knife and Eggcup
C.A.S. 1978

Bread, Jug and Eggcup c.1979 23 x 37cm
Chelmsford and Essex Museum 1979

Breadknife and Teaspoons c.1970s 34 x 20 cm Pl.128
Breakfast – wash drawing 1942
The Hilton Gallery 1948

Breakfast Things 1970 35.25 x 20cm
C.A.S. 1972; The Minories 1973

Broom – line and colour drawing 1944
The Hilton Gallery 1948

Candle 1973 24 x 41cm
Castle Museum Norwich 1974; University of Keele 1976; Chelmsford and Essex Museum 1979

Chair and Coat 1973 51 x 31cm
The Minories/Castle Museum 1973/74

Chairs and Candles 1986 34.5 x 31cm
Drawings for All 1986; Gainsborough's House, Sudbury, Suffolk; Collection Ipswich Borough Museums and Galleries (1987)

Chairs and Coat 1973 33 x 36cm
The Minories 1973

Chairs, Coat and Boots 1973 34.5 x 21.5cm
Castle Museum Norwich 1974; Chelmsford and Essex Museum 1979

Clown 1970 32 x 12.5cm
The Minories 1973

Cocoa – wash drawing 1942
The Hilton Gallery 1948

Conversation Piece – charcoal drawing 1994 90 x 65cm
Corn Poppy – line and colour drawing 1944
The Hilton Gallery 1948

Cow Parsnip – line and colour drawing 1944
The Hilton Gallery 1948

Deserted House with Two Jeering Characters – charcoal
C.A.S. 2000

Don Quixote and Sanzo Panza VII 1947
The Hilton Gallery 1948

Dustbin Lid with Pail 46 x 66cm
Figure with Candles 1972 76 x 31cm
The Minories 1973

Figures Playing – charcoal
C.A.S. 1985

Garden 1973 53 x 64cm
Castle Museum Norwich 1974

Garden at Stanway 1970 52 x 63.5cm
The Minories 1973

Ground Ivy – line and colour drawing 1944
The Hilton Gallery 1948

Group – wash drawing 1942
The Hilton Gallery 1948

Hare Bell – line and colour drawing 1942
The Hilton Gallery 1948

Hat and Boots 1973 14 x 27cm
The Minories 1973; C.A.S. 1975

Hatted Player 1972 15 x 36cm
The Minories/Castle Museum Norwich 1973/74; Chelmsford and Essex Museum 1979; The Minories/Playhouse Gallery 1984 C.A.S. Spons.

Hatted Players
C.A.S. 1993

Jawbone, Hat and Plimsoles 1973 23 x 34.5cm
Castle Museum Norwich 1974

Jonathan and Jenny
C.A.S. 1996

Jug 1973 23 x27cm
Castle Museum Norwich 1974

Jug and Bread 1974 25 x35cm Pl.144
The Minories/Castle Museum Norwich 1973/74; C.A.S. 1973, 1978; Chelmsford and Essex Museum 1979; The Playhouse Gallery 1984, C.A.S. Spons.; Christchurch Mansion 1987; Chappel Galleries, 1991

Jug and Candle 1973 38 x 25cm
Castle Museum Norwich1974; I & J Weiss 1976; Chelmsford and Essex Museum 1979

Jug and Papers 1974 36 x 20cm Pl.125
Jug and Plate 1972 36 x 43cm
The Minories 1973, 1996

Jug and Tea Cosy c.1973 23 x 33cm Pl.143
Jug, Hat, Candle and Boots
C.A.S. 1981

Jugs 1973 23 x 27cm Pl.103
The Minories 1984, C.A.S. Spons.; C.A.S. 1986

Lady's Smock – line and colour drawing 1944
The Hilton Gallery 1948

Lane at Stanway 1971 32 x 24cm
The Minories/Castle Museum Norwich 1973/74

Lesser St John's Wort – line and colour drawing 1944
The Hilton Gallery 1948

Man and Wheelbarrow 1971 44.5 x 61cm
The Minories 1973

Man and Wheelbarrow 1972 28 x 36cm
The Minories 1973

Man and Wheelbarrow 1972 20 x 31cm
The Minories 1973, C.A.S. Spons.

Man and Wheelbarrow 1973 46 x 61cm
Castle Museum Norwich 1974

Man and Wheelbarrow 25 x 31cm
The Minories 1984, C.A.S. Spons.

Milk Jug 25 x 36cm
Oxford Gallery 1971

Morning Table 1970 37 x 25cm
Oxford Gallery 1971; The Minories/Castle Museum Norwich 1973/74

Morning Table 38 x 51cm
Chelmsford Museum 1979

Narrow Leaved Vetch – line and colour drawing 1944
The Hilton Gallery 1948

Nipplewort – line and colour drawing 1944
The Hilton Gallery 1948

Norah Johns Dr 25 x 20cm
The Minories/Playhouse Gallery Harlow 1984, C.A.S. Spons; Christchurch Mansion 1987

Oak Stump with Ivy – pencil drawing 1946
The Hilton Gallery 1948

Off the Street – wash drawing 1942
The Hilton Gallery 1948

Paper and Candle 1973 23 x 41cm Pl.126
C.A.S. 1983; The Minories/Playhouse Gallery Harlow 1984, C.A.S. Spons.

Plimsoles, Hat and Bone 36 x 25cm
The Minories/Playhouse Gallery Harlow 1984, C.A.S. Spons.

Ronald Atkin 25 x 20cm
The Minories/Playhouse Gallery Harlow 1984, C.A.S. Spons.

Round Table 1970 32 x 24cm
The Minories/Castle Museum Norwich 1973/74; Chelmsford and Essex Museum 1979

St. John's Wort – line and colour drawing 1944
The Hilton Gallery 1948

Salt Cellar and Bread 20 x 28cm
The Minories/Playhouse Gallery Harlow 1984, C.A.S. Spons.; C.A.S. 1997

Skull, Hat and Boots 1973 19 x 39.5cm
The Minories 1973; I & J Weiss 1976; Chelmsford and Essex Museum 1979; The Minories 1979, 'Essex and Suffolk Artists 1900-1978

Sleeper – wash drawing 1942
The Hilton Gallery 1948

Sleeping Child 1944
The Hilton Gallery 1948

Sleeping Child 20 x 31cm
(lent by L. Barrett)
The Minories 1984, C.A.S. Spons.

Sleeping Child 1944
The Hilton Gallery 1948

Sleeping Child 25 x 33cm
Christchurch Mansion 1987

Still Life 18 x 37cm
The Minories/Playhouse Gallery Harlow 1984, C.A.S. Spons.

Student 1962 24 x 19cm
The Minories/Castle Museum Norwich 1973/74; The Minories 1984, C.A.S. Spons.

Table and Chairs c.1970s 36 x 34cm Pl.102
Oxford Gallery 1971

Tea Cosy 1970 38 x 20cm
Oxford Gallery 1971; C.A.S. 1971; The Minories/Castle Museum Norwich 1973/74; University of Keele 1976; Chelmsford and Essex Museum 1979

Trees 1971 31 x 23cm
The Minories/Castle Museum Norwich 1973/1974; C.A.S. 1979; The Minories/Playhouse Gallery Harlow 1984, C.A.S. Spons.; Christchurch Mansion 1987

Umbrella Man I 1974 42 x 19cm
Castle Museum Norwich 1974

Umbrella Man II 1974 52 x 26.5cm
Warehouse Cellar – wash drawing 1942
The Hilton Gallery 1948

Wood Dog Violet – line and colour drawing 1944
The Hilton Gallery 1948

Yellow Toad Flax – line and colour drawing 1944
The Hilton Gallery 1948

Note: all pencil unless otherwise stated.

PRINTS 1934–56

After Bellini – wood engraving | 1937 | 28 x 21cm | not known | Pl.246
All That Should Be | 1938 | 18 x 11.5cm | not known | Pl.255
– wood engraving
Ass and Man – wood engraving | 1951 | 18.5 x 17cm | Ed.50 | Pl.270
black version
Ed.12 | Pl.269
yellow version

C.A.S. Colchester Castle, 1951; Society of Wood Engravers 1951; Beaux Arts Gallery, 1954; The Lamont Gallery, 1957; King Street Gallery, Cambridge, 1963; University of Keele, 1976; Chelmsford & Essex Museum, 1979; The Minories, 1984; Meeanee Barracks, 1992; The Minories/Castle Museum, Norwich, 1973/74; Chappel Galleries, 1991; published 20th Century British Wood Engravers 1997 by Hal Bishop

Autumn | 1938 | not known | not known
Beech – wood engraving | c.1951 | 8 x 13cm | | Pl.276
Behold the Mother and Child | 1938–40 | 12 x 9cm | not known | Pl.258
– linocut
Bicycle Family see Family Bike Ride
Big Sad Dog – wood engraving | 1938 | 18 x 11.5cm | Ed.6 | Pl.253
The Hilton Gallery, 1948
Bike Ride – linocut | c.1956 | 22 x 13.5cm | Ed.3 | Pl.287
King Street Gallery, Cambridge, 1963; The Minories, 1973/Castle Museum Norwich, 1973/74
Birthday Cake – wood engraving | c.1950s | 15.5 x 13cm | not known | Pl.289
Blue Bird (The) – wood engraving | 1940 | 18.5 x 17cm | Ed.25 | Pl.264
The Hilton Gallery, 1948; published in 20th Century British Wood Engravers 1997
Boy – wood engraving | 1939 | 15 x 23cm | not known | Pl.256
The Hilton Gallery, 1948; Society of Wood Engravers 1939–40
Boy Asleep – wood engraving | 1938 | 23 x 15cm | Ed.7 | Pl.254
Boy with Girl – wood engraving | c.1937 | 10 x 14cm | not known | Pl.241
Bridge Over Stream | c.1937 | 14 x 10cm | not known | Pl.229
– wood engraving
Cecil Barrett – wood engraving | c.1930 | 5.5 x 5cm | not known | Pl.202
Chairs and Men – wood engraving | 1952 | 26.5 x 20cm | Ed.50 | Pl.278
Xylon I 1953; Beaux Arts Gallery, London, 1954; King Street Gallery, Cambridge, 1963; The Minories/Castle Museum, Norwich, 1973/74; The Lamont Gallery, 1975; University of Keele, 1976; The Minories, 1984/C.A.S. spons.; published 'Studio' November 1963; Meeanee Barracks 1992; Collection Victoria and Albert Museum; published in 20th Century British Wood Engravers 1997 by Hal Bishop

Cobbett's Rural Rides 1937 – wood engravings
Village | 8.5 x 11cm | not known | Pl.238
Farmer Leading Horse | 7.5 x 11cm | not known | Pl.234
Two Men and Cart Horse | 7.5 x 11cm | not known | Pl.235
Men Carrying Sacks | 6.5 x 11cm | not known | Pl.236
Men Going Through Door | 7.5 x 11cm | not known | Pl.237
Farmer on Horse with Two Trees | 5 x 8.5cm | not known | Pl.232
Farmer on Horse | 5 x 7.5cm | not known | Pl.233
Farmstead | 14 x 11cm | not known | Pl.230
Two Figures on Hill above | 14 x 11cm | not known | Pl.231
Farmstead
Cock and Fox – wood engraving | c.1950s | 11.5 x 17.5cm | not known | Pl.283
Published in 20th Century British Wood Engravers 1997
Deserted House with Two | 1955 | 30 x 40cm | Ed.15 | Pl.286
Leering Characters – linocut (2 colour)
Beaux Arts Gallery, 1956; Xylon II 1957; The Lamont Gallery, USA 1957; The Minories/Castle Museum, Norwich 1973/74; The Minories, 1984; C.A.S. sponsored; Society of Wood Engravers 1955
Dogwood – wood engraving | c.1951 | 18 x 8cm | not known | Pl.277
Society of Wood Engravers 1952

Don Quixote and Cock | 1950 | 19.5 x 6.5cm | not known | Pl.267
– wood engraving
Don Quixote and Sancho Panza | 1939–40 | 20 x 13cm | not known | Pl.257
– wood engraving
Dog Rose – wood engraving | c.1951 | 8 x 13cm | not known | Pl.274
Drink by Candlelight | c.1937 | 12.5 x 18cm | not known | Pl.240
– wood engraving
Eight Figures – linocut | c.1937 | 28 x 21cm | not known | Pl.244
Engraving for War Poem | 1937 | 10 x 14cm | Ed.7 | Pl.239
– wood engraving
Father, Mother, Child | 1939–40 | size unknown | not known | Pl.259
– wood engraving
Fallen Chair – wood engraving | 1956 | 20 x 26cm | Ed.15 | Pl.288
A/p Ed.16

Beaux Arts Gallery, 1956; The Lamont Gallery, USA 1957; Society of Wood Engravers 1955; King Street Gallery, 1963; The Minories/Castle Museum, Norwich, 1973/74; Chelmsford and Essex Museum, 1979; The Minories 1984; published in 20th Century British Wood Engravers 1997 by Hal Bishop

Family Bike Ride – wood engraving | 1952 | 18 x 8cm | not known | Pl.279
Beaux Arts Gallery 1954; The Lamont Gallery, USA, 1957; Collection of the Victoria and Albert Museum
Family House – wood engraving | 1952 | 7.5 x 7cm | Ed.20 | Pl.280
Society of Wood Engravers 1953; Xylon I 1953; The Lamont Gallery, USA 1957
Family of Chairs – wood engraving | 1950–55 | 6 x 9.5cm | not known | Pl.281
The Lamont Gallery, USA, 1957; Castle Museum, Norwich, 1974
Falstaff, Henry IV – wood engraving | 1938 | 18 x 12cm | Ed.3 | Pl.248
Figure – linocut | 1949 | 27 x 26.5cm | Ed.20 | Pl.268
Five Candles – wood engraving | c.1950s | 7 x 11.5cm | not known | Pl.252
Five Figures – lino/woodcut | 1936–37 | 28 x 20cm | not known | Pl.227
Four Figures in the style of | 1938 | 18 x 11cm | | Pl.249
Henry IV – wood engraving
Group with Sun – woodcut | c.1936 | 10 x 8cm | not known | Pl.213
Head with Five Figures – linocut | c.1937 | 29 x 23cm | not known | Pl.247
Henry IV – wood engraving | 1938 | 8 x 11.5cm | | Pl.251
Henry IV (7 Figures) | 1938 | 18 x 12cm | not known | Pl.250
– wood engraving
Journey – wood engraving | 1951 | 19.5 x 25cm | Ed.45 | Pl.271
Society of Wood Engravers 1951, 87; Xylon I 1953; Beaux Arts Gallery, 1954; The Lamont Gallery, USA, 1957; Gainsborough's House, 1962; King Street Gallery, Cambridge, 1963; The Minories/Castle Museum, Norwich, 1973/74; Chelmsford & Essex Museum, 1979; The Minories, 1984; Chappel Galleries, 1991; Meeanee Barracks, 1992; published 20th Century British Wood Engravers 1997 by Hal Bishop
King and Candle – wood engraving | c.1950s | 7 x 7.5cm | Ed.10 | Pl.284
King Herod and the Cock – linocut | 1946 | 30.5 x 23.5cm | Ed.50 | Pl.260
(black version)
Ed.50 | Pl.261
(red version)
unknown | Pl.262
(brown version)

The Hilton Gallery, 1948

Landscape – lino/woodcut | c.1936 | 9 x 5cm | not known | Pl.216
Large and Small Figure | c.1936 | 29 x 23cm | not known | Pl.214
– lino/woodcut
Love – etching | 1939 | 15 x 17cm | Ed.6 | Pl.263
Man and Plant – wood engraving | 1936–37 | 14 x 10cm | not known | Pl.223
Man Hailing Weather | 1936–37 | 12 x 10cm | not known | Pl.226
– wood engraving
Man in Pond – woodcut/engraving | 1936 | 15.5 x 10cm | not known | Pl.220

Man in Swirl – wood engraving | 1936–37 | 15 x 10cm | not known | Pl.225
Man in Tempest – woodcut | c.1936 | 13 x 10cm | not known | Pl.210
Man in Trees – lino/woodcut | c.1935 | 8 x 9cm | not known | Pl.209
Man in the Woods (A) | c.1936 | 9 x 8cm | not known | Pl.215
– lino/woodcut
Man looking up Tree | 1936 | 10 x 7.5cm | not known | Pl.218
– wood engraving
Man with Aura – wood engraving | 1936–37 | 17.5 x 12.5cm | not known | Pl.224
Man with Book – lino/woodcut | c.1935 | 19 x 14cm | not known | Pl.208
Mr A and Mr B – not known | not known | not known | not known
Painter – wood engraving | 1948 | 18 x 11.5cm | Ed.50 | Pl.266
Published 20th Century British Wood Engravers 1997 by Hal Bishop
Patriarch – lino/woodcut | c.1936 | 13 x 8 cm | not known | Pl.217
Sleeping Chair | 1950–55 | 13.5 x 22.5cm | Ed.2 | Pl.282
– wood engraving | then Ed.7
Beaux Arts Gallery, 1956; King Street Gallery, 1963; The Minories, 1984
Spindle – wood engraving | c.1951 | 18 x 8cm | | Pl.275
Published by Agricultural Contractors Ltd Calendar
Striding – linocut | 1934–35 | 7 x 6.5cm | not known | Pl.203
Strongman – linocut | 1934–35 | 11.5 x 8.5cm | not known | Pl.204
St Christopher Magazine 1935 | 1935 | 30 x 22cm | | Pl.206
St Christopher Magazine July 1935 | 1935 | 30 x 22cm | | Pl.207
Summer – not known | not known | not known | not known
Society of Wood Engravers 1939–40
Tombstones – wood engraving | 1937 | 15.5 x 10cm | not known | Pl.228
Tramp – wood engraving | 1936 | 6.5 x 5cm | not known | Pl.221
Traveller – wood engraving | 1947 | 10 x 13.5cm | Ed.14 | Pl.265
Published 20th Century British Wood Engravers 1997 by Hal Bishop
Tree and Diagonal River – woodcut | c.1936 | 15 x 11cm | not known | Pl.212
Tree with Fence – lino/woodcut | c.1935–36 | 18 x 13cm | not known | Pl.211
Two Angels and Man | 1936 | 12 x 11cm | not known | Pl.219
– wood engraving
Two Farmworkers | 1936–37 | 16 x 12.5cm | not known | Pl.222
– wood engraving
Two Heads Outline – lino/woodcut | c.1950s | 9.5 x 12.5cm | not known | Pl.285
Two Men Gesticulating – linocut | 1935 | not known | not known | Pl.205
Two Tragic Figures – Lear | 1937 | 14 x 7.5cm | not known | Pl.245
– wood engraving
Visitor – wood engraving | c.1950s | 13.5 x 7cm | not known | Pl.290
Whitebeam – wood engraving | c.1951 | 8 x 13cm | not known | Pl.272
Published by Agricultural Contractors Ltd Calendar
Woman – wood engraving | c.1937 | 14 x 10cm | not known | Pl.242
Woodland Forms | c.1937 | 6 x 5cm | not known | Pl.243
– wood engraving
Yew – wood engraving | c.1951 | 19 x 8cm | not known | Pl.273

Notes:
International Society of Wood Engravers Exhibitions
Xylon I 1953: Zurich
Xylon II 1956–57: Zurich, Ljubliana, Berlin, Wuppertal, Portogruaro, Nancy and Vienna

Where prints are editioned and/or have been exhibited, it can be taken that these have titles ascribed by Roderic himself, otherwise the editor has given a working title as an identifier only.

LIST OF EXHIBITIONS BY DATE

1939–40 Society of Wood Engravers

1946 C.A.S. Colchester Castle

1946-52 Donovan Rowley Gallery, Swan Passage, Colchester: exhibitions with B. Hugh-Stanton, C. Morris, J. Nash, F. Harnack, A. Blundell, E. Watson, H. & J. Collins, J. K. Popham, R. Suddaby, J. Graham. Nelson Blowers was apprenticed to Donovan Rowley, eventually setting up as an independent framer to artists in the region, including Michael Chase, Peter Coker RA, Valerie Thornton. He was to be Roderic Barrett's framer for fifty years.)

1947 C.A.S. Colchester Castle

1948 The Hilton Gallery, St. Mary's Passage, Cambridge: solo: 26 April – 1 May

1949 C.A.S. Colchester Castle

1950 C.A.S. Colchester Castle: Spring, Autumn

1951 C.A.S. Colchester Castle: Autumn

1951 Society of Wood Engravers

1952 C.A.S. Colchester Castle: Autumn

1952 Society of Wood Engravers

1953 C.A.S. Colchester Castle

1953 Society of Wood Engravers

1953 International Society of Wood Engravers, Xylon I, Zurich

1954 Beaux Arts Gallery, Bruton Place London W.: solo (also John Bratby solo): 16 September – 16 October

1955 C.A.S. Colchester Castle

1955 Society of Wood Engravers

1956 C.A.S. Colchester Castle: Spring, Autumn

1956 Beaux Arts Gallery, Bruton Place, London W.1: solo: 16 June – 16 July

1956–57 International Society of Wood Engravers, Xylon II, Zurich, Ljubliana, Berlin, Wuppertal, Portogruaro, Nancy, Vienna

1957 C.A.S. Colchester Castle: Spring

1957 The Lamont Gallery, Phillips Exeter Academy, Exeter, N.H., USA: solo: 16 September – 5 October

1958 Shore Studio Galleries, 167 Newbury Street, Boston USA: solo: 5–22 February

1958 Boston Arts Festival, Boston, USA

1958 C.A.S. The Minories Colchester: Autumn

1959 C.A.S. Colchester Castle: Spring; The Minories, Colchester: Autumn

1961 C.A.S. The Minories, Colchester:

1961 Wildenstein & Co. Ltd., 147 New Bond Street, London W.1: Roderic Barrett, Brian Crouch, Geoffrey Genever, Caroline Leeds, Roman Black, Connie Fenn, Margaret Kroch-Fisherman, Garrick Palmer, Edward Wakeford: 22 February – 18 March

1961 Gainsborough's House, Sudbury, Suffolk Winter Exhibition: 16 December – 9 January

1961 Gainsborough's House: Joyce Pallot, Henry Collins, Roderic Barrett: 16 December – 9 January

1962 C.A.S. The Minories, Colchester/Colchester Castle; Spring/Autumn The Minories, Colchester: solo

1963 King Street Gallery, Cambridge: solo: 26 April – 11 May

1964 Holland Park Gallery, London: Roderic Barrett, Hugh MacKinnon 27 April – May 27

1965 The Minories, Colchester/Colchester Castle: Spring/Autumn

1966 C.A.S. The Minories, Colchester: Spring

1966 Alwin Gallery 56 Brook Street London W.1: solo: May

1966 Alwin Gallery, London (painting Three Part Dance) 1966

1966 The Hilton Gallery, Trumpington Street, Cambridge: solo: 7–21 November

1966 University of Essex : solo

1967 C.A.S. The Minories, Colchester

1967 Alwin Gallery, 56 Brook Street London W.1: solo: 4–28 October

1968 C.A.S. The Minories, Colchester: Summer

1969 C.A.S. The Minories, Colchester/Colchester Castle: Spring/Autumn

1969 Free Painters and Sculptors, Quantas Gallery, London; New Fellows Exhibition: April, Long Melford

1970 Alwin Gallery, 56 Brook Street London W.1: solo: 3–27 June

1970 Royal Academy, London: Summer Exhibition

1970 C.A.S. Colchester Castle: Autumn

1970 Graves Art Gallery, Sheffield: Open Art Exhibition: November

c.1970 Ash Barn Gallery, Stroud, Hants

1971 C.A.S. Colchester Castle/The Minories, Colchester: Summer/Winter

1971 Oxford Gallery, 23 High Street, Oxford: solo: 4 July – 4 August

1971 Royal Academy, London: Summer Exhibition

1971 Ipswich

1972 C.A.S. Colchester Castle: Summer

1972 Royal Academy, London: Summer Exhibition

1973 C.A.S. Colchester Castle: Spring

1973 Royal Academy, London: Summer Exhibition

1973 The Minories, Colchester: Roderic Barrett's "Measure" A Retrospective: 14 October – 11 November

1974 C.A.S. The Minories, Colchester: Winter

1974 Castle Museum, Norwich: Roderic Barrett's "Measure" A Retrospective: March

1974 Royal Academy, London: Summer Exhibition

1975 University of Southampton: solo

1975 Oxford Gallery, 23 High Street, Oxford: Roderic Barrett and Valerie Thornton

1975 C.A.S. Colchester Castle/The Minories, Colchester: Summer/Winter

1976 University of Keele; Chancellor's Building: solo: 16 April – 14 May

1976 Playhouse Gallery, The High, Harlow: solo: 28 May – 21 June

1976 I & J Weiss, 57a Priory Street, Colchester, Essex: Anthony Atkinson, Roderic Barrett, Charles Bartlett, Peter Coker RA, Henry Collins, John Dann, William Garfitt, Olwen Jones, Joyce Pallott, Valerie Thornton, Ivor Weiss, Richard Whitehouse: 7 – 21 June

1976 Royal Academy, London: Summer Exhibition

1976 Thackeray Gallery, London: solo: 29 September – 15 October

1976 C.A.S. The Minories, Colchester: Winter

1977 Playhouse Gallery, The High, Harlow, Essex: The First Five Years: Henry Moore, Jessie Watkins, John Piper, Roderic Barrett, Alan Burgess, Alan Davies, Frank Fidler, Jane Humphreys, William Mills, Michael O'Connell, Arnold Van Praag: 1–30 April

1977 Royal Academy, London: Summer Exhibition

1977 C.A.S. The Minories, Colchester: Winter

1978 Royal Academy, London: Summer Exhibition

1978 Thackeray Gallery, London: solo: 18 October – 3 November

1979 The Minories, Colchester: Essex and Suffolk Artists: J. Armstrong, M. Ayrton, R. Barrett, E. Bawden, R. Bedford, A. Boyd, G. Clarke, P. Coker, L. Freud, L. Haines, J. Herman, E. Middleditch, C. Morris, A. Munnings, J. Nash, E. Paolozzi, L. Pissarro, M. Potter, E. Ravilious, J. Ridgewell, C. Rogers, M. Rothenstein, V. Thornton, K. Vaughan: 31 March – April 29

1979 Chelmsford & Essex Museum C.A.S. Sponsored: solo: 26 May – 18 July

1979 Royal Academy, London: Summer Exhibition

1979 The Digby Gallery, Mercury Theatre, Colchester: solo: November

1980 Royal Academy, London: Summer Exhibition

1980 Thackeray Gallery, London: solo: 24 September – 10 October

1980 C.A.S. The Minories, Colchester: Winter

1981 Royal Academy, London: Summer Exhibition

1981 C.A.S. The Minories, Colchester: Winter

1982 Royal Academy, London: Summer Exhibition

1982 C.A.S. The Minories, Colchester

1983 Phoenix Gallery, 99 High St, Lavenham, Suffolk: Spring Mixed Exhibition: April C.A.S. Colchester Castle/The Minories, Colchester: Spring/Winter

1983 Royal Academy, London: Summer Exhibition

1983 Oxford Gallery

1984 C.A.S. Colchester Castle/The Minories, Colchester: Spring/Winter

1984 Royal Academy, London: Summer Exhibition

1984 The Minories, Colchester: Roderic Barrett and Bernard Reynolds; C.A.S. Sponsored: 21 July – 21 August

1984 The Playhouse Gallery, The High, Harlow, Essex: Solo: 18 October – 10 November

1985 C.A.S. Colchester Castle/The Minories Colchester: Spring/Winter

1985 Royal Academy, London: Summer Exhibition

1986 C.A.S. Colchester Castle/The Minories, Colchester: Spring/Winter

1986 Royal Academy, London: Summer Exhibition

1987 Society of Wood Engravers

1987 Christchurch Mansion, Ipswich, Suffolk: Solo: 18 April – 25 May

1987 Royal Academy, London: Summer Exhibition

1987 C.A.S. Beecroft Art Gallery, Westcliff-on-Sea, Essex/The Minories, Colchester: Autumn/Winter

1988 C.A.S. Colchester Castle/The Minories, Colchester: Spring/Winter

1988 Epping Forest District Museum: Artists in Essex: Work purchased: 25 May – June 13

1988 Royal Academy, London: Summer Exhibition

1988 Phoenix Gallery, 99 High Street, Lavenham, Suffolk: Solo: 29 October – November 21

1989 C.A.S. The Digby Gallery, Colchester: Honorary Members/Colchester Castle: Spring/Framing Centre, Colchester

1989 Royal Academy, London: Summer Exhibition, Beecroft Art Gallery, Westcliff-on-Sea, Essex; Epping Forest District Museum: Artists in Essex, Chappel Galleries, Essex

1990 Beecroft Art Gallery, Westcliff-on-Sea: Solo: 24 March – 21 April

1990 Chappel Galleries, Essex: Spring Exhibition: 6–27 May

1990 C.A.S. Colchester Castle/Framing Centre, East Hill, Colchester: Spring/Summer; Quay Theatre Open

1990 Fermoy Gallery and Red Barn Gallery, King's Lynn Art Centre, Norfolk: Eastern Open (highly commended by Derrick Greaves, Gillian and Neville Jason)

1990 Chappel Galleries, Essex: Christmas Exhibition: 9–24 December

1991 Chappel Galleries, Essex: Prints and Drawings: 3–24 February

1991 Fermoy Gallery and Red Barn Gallery, King's Lynn Art Centre, Norfolk: Eastern Open

1991 Royal Academy, London: Summer Exhibition